A Guide to
Caravanning & Camping
in South Africa

James Berrangé

STRUIK

First published in 1999 by Struik Publishers (Pty) Ltd
(a member of Struik New Holland Publishing (Pty) Ltd)
London • Cape Town • Sydney • Auckland

24 Nutford Place
London W1H 6DQ
United Kingdom

14 Aquatic Drive
Frenchs Forest
NSW 2086, Australia

80 McKenzie Street
Cape Town 8001
South Africa

218 Lake Road
Northcote, Auckland
New Zealand

Reg. no: 54/00965/07

2 4 6 8 10 9 7 5 3 1

Copyright © 1999 in published edition: Struik Publishers (Pty) Ltd
Copyright © 1999 in text: James Berrangé
Copyright © 1999 cover photograph: David Steele/Photo Access

Managing editor: Lesley Hay-Whitton
Cover design: Tracey Mackenzie
Designers: Tracey Mackenzie and Petal Palmer
Editor: Gail Jennings
Typesetters: Illana Fridkin and Petal Palmer
Proofreader and indexer: Claudia Dos Santos

ISBN 1 86872 319 4

Reproduction by Disc Express Cape (Pty) Ltd
Printed and bound by CTP Book Printers (Pty) Ltd,
Caxton Street, Parow 7500, Cape Town

All rights reserved. No part of this publication may be reproduced,
stored in a retrieval system or transmitted, in any form or by
any means, electronic, mechanical, photocopying or
otherwise, without the prior written permission of the
publishers and copyright holders.

ACKNOWLEDGEMENTS

There are many people to whom I owe a debt of thanks, some of whom were simply fellow holidaymakers I met while travelling, but who were nevertheless always friendly and more than willing to take a few extra minutes to trade ideas with me. However insignificant these passing moments might have seemed, it was this constant cross-pollination of thoughts and ideas that built the enthusiasm for further refinement and creation. Among this group I would include several Department of Nature Conservation officials, local inhabitants of various small towns, and owners of resorts.

At Struik I would like to give special thanks to Mariëlle Renssen, Annlerie van Rooyen and Lesley Hay-Whitton for words of encouragement and guidance, and to Tracey Mackenzie for a great design. Gail Jennings, a fellow camper, did some skilful editing, asked all the right questions and made many useful suggestions.

I am perhaps deepest in debt to ex-colleague Chris Whales for steering me in the right direction (to McKenzie Street, in Cape Town). Without his disarming manner and 'direct-route' thinking, this book might never have found its way to its publisher.

Lastly I would like to thank the 'invisible heroes' of publishing, namely the men and women in typesetting, repro, printing, distribution and marketing for their considerable efforts in bringing this publication to final fruition.

James Berrangé
Cape Town 1999

CONTENTS

CHAPTER ONE – PLANNING THE TRIP   8
In search of a destination (Large resorts; The purpose-built caravan park; National parks; Wilderness, bush or mountain camps); Booking your spot; Before you leave home; Equipment; Leaving the resort; Back at home

CHAPTER TWO – LIFE IN A CAR   17
Reading the road; In-house entertainment; Under the sun; Comfort zone; Maps

CHAPTER THREE – TENTS   23
'Play' tents; Cottage tents; Dome tents; Frame tents; Other types of tents; Pegs, zips and spares

CHAPTER FOUR – TRAILERS   30
Nose cones; Wheels; Suspension; Mudguards; Luggage racks; Trailer variations

CHAPTER FIVE – CARAVANS   36
The two-berth caravan; The four- to-six berth caravan; Personal space; Storage space; Colour; Windows; Power; The galley; Ventilation; Sleeping arrangements; Water; Air conditioning; Shade; Tents; Getting organised; Packing; Safety on the road (The view ahead; Traffic; Mirrors and stabiliser bars; Suspension; Gear ratios; Speed; Braking; Overtaking)

CHAPTER SIX – MOTORHOMES   55
Diesel technology; Camper units; Camper 'vans'; Medium-sized motorhomes; Interior layouts; Increasing your mobility; Caring for your second home

CHAPTER SEVEN – LIGHTING   61
Candles; Hurricane lamps; Pressure lamps; Gas; Electricity; Torches; Light sticks

CHAPTER EIGHT – THE OUTDOOR KITCHEN 66
Fixed stoves; Portable gas stoves; Pressure stoves; No-pressure stoves; Fridges and freezers; Eating out (Tables; Chairs; Setting the table); Kitchen utensils (Knives; Sharpening implements; Other 'must-have' devices); Outdoor cooking implements (The cooking grid; The cast-iron potjie; The skottel; Crockery and utensils); The open fire (Making a fire; Fire wood; Compressed fuel; Safety)

CHAPTER NINE – SLEEPING 92
What to sleep on; What to sleep in; What to sleep under

CHAPTER TEN – CLOTHING 95
Headgear; Jackets and jerseys; Shirts, pants, socks and shoes; Winter clothing; Sunglasses

CHAPTER ELEVEN – STORAGE 99
Clothing; Toiletries; Food (Dry foods; Wet foods); Water; Fuel and distillates

CHAPTER TWELVE – ACCESSORIES 104
Protection from the elements; Tables and chairs; Braai units; Other accessories

CHAPTER THIRTEEN – CAMPING WITH CHILDREN 110
Before you leave home; On the road; Fears and dangers

CHAPTER FOURTEEN – 'SURVIVAL' 116
Snakes; Malaria; Stings and bites; Poisonous plants; Shellfish; Your emergency box

CHAPTER FIFTEEN – ABLUTIONS & CAMP ETiQUETTE 122
Ablution blocks; Riverside safety; Bush etiquette; Music; Simple good manners

APPENDICES 126
Shops, Clubs and Magazines
Caravan Parks; Index

INTRODUCTION

There was once a perception out there that camping was the poor person's holiday; caravanning was for the not-so-poor, but if money was no problem we would all stay in luxury hotels.

Few ideas about the outdoors could be more incorrect. To be quite honest, though, budget is a crucial consideration when it comes to travelling, and very little can beat a camping trip for good value. If you know – and have – the basics, there's no need to 'rough it' too much, either.

Every aspect of outdoor living and holidaying has its own fascination – and every form of accommodation its own appeal. For many first-time campers, sitting on the ground with a plate on your lap is satisfying in its simplicity and entertaining in its novelty. And it provides happy memories and, particularly for the young, a reference point for things to come. But like other 'romantic' ideas, such as sleeping on Mother Earth and taking cold showers, the thought can be more creditable than the reality.

In this guide you'll discover the many outdoor holidaying options – I have tried not to use the word 'advantage' when describing any of them, as this implies that one is better than another, which is not necessarily the case. 'Better than' depends very much on what you wanted in the first place.

To the dedicated camper, anything 'less' than canvas flapping in the wind may be second best; to the motorhome enthusiast a car and caravan may appear as a strange creature suffering from arrested evolution; to the caravan owner, neither of the two come close to the comfort and convenience of the car and caravan combination.

Anyone planning an outdoor vacation in South Africa will be faced with many choices, which can become quite bewildering. Some choices revolve around the purchase of equipment, but an equal number may involve methods, venues and countless other aspects of outdoor living. Fortunately, the outdoor industry is not plagued by shortages and the aspirant outdoor enthusiast will be able to pick and choose to his or her heart's content.

But often this vast range presents a problem of its own. What to buy? How much to spend? What is essential and what can comfortably be left at home? What did we use last time? This guide should provide some of the answers.

Dealing with known quantities and exploiting each and every situation to the maximum is the key to giving everyone a good time while having one yourself.

Planning a holiday should be a group activity that creates a joyful air of expectancy. Remember, too, that the quality of a vacation also depends on others, and at the end of a season resort owners look to their customers to tell them whether their expectations have been met. The more organised resorts may even ask you to fill in a questionnaire on departure; put aside time to fill it in honestly and thoughtfully. Your feedback is a vital element in providing satisfaction.

We hope this guide will contribute to many happy days and weeks outdoors and many happy memories. Enjoy.

CHAPTER ONE

PLANNING THE TRIP

Like most things in life, what you get out of an activity is in direct proportion to what you put into it from the start. Vacation time is a precious commodity and it's worth going that extra mile so that everyone gets the most out of the time spent away from home.

IN SEARCH OF A DESTINATION

The first decision is obviously where to go. The most important factor here is geography – and how it has been exploited for your advantage. Coastal destinations are fine if you live inland, but people who live close to the sea may hanker after something different. In South Africa we have a wonderful variety of recreational places, and although many offer similar-sounding activities, the experiences can be very different for each one.

Finding a destination that has something for everyone is not easy. Nightclubs, gyms, TV rooms and waterslides may well be a teenage paradise (and give mum and dad snatches of peace and quiet), but will probably be meaningless to a young couple in search of a tranquil setting. So don't try to find everything in one resort, although for any group to exist happily together there does need to be some binding interest. You may reach a decision more easily if you decide what you don't want: game-viewing may be a hit with the tourists but locals may have had the experience many times.

Once you have a place in mind, find out more about it, either by getting in touch with someone who has spent some time there or by speaking to the proprietors.

Find out, for example, about the attitudes and personalities of the

BEFORE YOU LEAVE...

■ Do you want to go on holiday as a family or in a group? The old saying about a problem shared is a problem halved is particularly true when it comes to holidays. People who visit the same resort every year invariably have friends who are there on arrival. Couples can take turns looking after children and so afford each other more time to pursue activities not appropriate for small children. Be careful about your choice of partners – bigger groups usually make for better dynamics.

■ Draw up a budget, even if you don't rigidly adhere to it. Build in things such as eating out or allowing younger ones to buy something of interest (which can be quite small) to take home.

■ Fraud has escalated wildly recently; many shop owners prefer to be paid in cash, so you need to carry some with you. Roadside vendors in rural areas usually cannot conclude a transaction any other way. Bear in mind that the smallest towns may not even have a bank, let alone an ATM, so plan accordingly.

■ Consider the length of the trip and break a long haul into several short ones. This doesn't mean that you can't do a meaningful number of kilometres every day – it simply means setting time aside for entertainment. Arriving relaxed the next day is infinitely preferable to arriving early but so exhausted that you need a day of recuperation before you can actually start enjoying yourself.

■ Refuelling is usually no problem on major routes. If you intend travelling further afield, where distances between towns and reliable garages are measured in hundreds of kilometres (in Namibia, for example), take extra fuel and water. A strong headwind or dust storm for several hours can wreak havoc with your fuel consumption, especially if you are towing a large caravan or heavy trailer.

management and staff members. And if you are planning to do a lot of hiking or have young family members who require many changes of clothing, there'll need to be a fully equipped laundry, including tumble dryers. If the washing gets done by camp staff (a small fee is usually in order), this may swing it for mother, who, apart from having an unofficial veto right on venues, will also have one less chore on her daily agenda. In terms of having a pleasant time, keeping mum happy is something worth fighting for!

Slightly older children and teenagers may find life boring (with dire consequences – the remedy of which goes way beyond the scope of this book) without some form of social activity to give it all meaning.

During hot summer days, a nearby large swimming pool where other children gather, play and form friendships can be a lifesaver.

Check out the cooking facilities, too. If you will be staying in a tent during the rainy season, ask whether there is a communal indoor cooking and washing-up facility. Not all resorts offer the cooking part, but those that do, such as the resort at Addo Elephant National Park, are worth remembering.

Ablution blocks are pretty much a standard feature of every resort, but not all will measure up to the highest standards. Most people expect to 'rough it' when living outdoors, and many see the minor inconveniences (such as an erratic hot-water supply) as half the fun. But still, it's worth finding out about.

Also look into the proximity of interesting shops, restaurants and other attractions, such as amusement parks, game reserves, art galleries, potters' studios or beaches, which can only add to the holiday experience. The local publicity office will be able to help with details.

Most park or resort shops supply basic consumables like bread, milk, toothpaste and firewood, but may not have a good supply of everything all the time, so ask about other sources close by.

LARGE RESORTS

These are not necessarily the first choice for everyone. They're highly developed, usually on prime land and are close to major tourist attractions, so they quite rightly pride themselves on being able to satisfy the most demanding holidaymaker. Accommodation may range from the simplest of camping sites, situated under shady indigenous trees, to luxurious fully serviced bungalows commanding views of the surrounding countryside. They may have several well laid-out ablution blocks so that no one has to walk too far or stand in a queue to shower or wash dishes. They may also offer a full gym, large pool, TV room, games room, trampolines and waterslides, and have a well-equipped shop and various pieces of recreational equipment for hire (or for free, with the cost built into the price of the site). Some even go so far as to hire minor celebrities who wander around from site to site in the evenings, joking with the guests and telling amusing stories!

THE PURPOSE-BUILT CARAVAN PARK

Because most visitors tow in their own accommodation, these hugely popular parks consist mainly of landscaped sites (of varying quality) on which to park the caravan. Purpose-built caravan parks often have no chalets or bungalows, and sometimes do not even allow tents, but may offer caravans for hire.

Before visiting such a venue for the first time, find out, for example, whether the sites are level, serviced (does someone remove waste?), and whether they are furnished with an electrical plug-in point (use is often optional). Is there a laundry service, and, if so, what does it consist of? If the laundrette is do-it-yourself, don't be afraid to ask about the number of washing machines and tumble dryers that are available and how far they are from your site. Lugging bags of laundry to and fro is not a sought-after holiday activity.

The degree of privacy on site is another important aspect and can vary greatly, depending on how important this aspect is to the owners of the park. Many do plant hedges or rows of shrubs to separate each site, but just as many have nothing at all.

In terms of cost, the biggest difference will be between the municipal resorts (which seem to be happy to exist the way they are as long as all the expenses are covered) and the private resorts (which are run much the same as any other business). New and developing resorts may plough back much of the profit into the resort; they know that the best way to improve the net worth of the place is to improve the appeal of their facilities. A high price, however, is not always a guarantee of quality, so don't let cost alone be the deciding factor.

PARKS AND RESERVES

For the over-stressed urbanite, there is not much to beat one of the many parks and reserves. Chosen for their uniqueness and purity of habitat, they offer South Africans a lot for comparatively little. The experience is essentially a bush one, providing the 'back-to-nature' feeling that's missing from the lives of many.

Cost of entry to a park or reserve is very much in the lower end of the price spectrum, and somehow there is great appeal in a venue where the main reason for its existence is not financial gain. The flora and fauna are often in overwhelming variety and abundance, and in addition there are usually education centres and friendly conservation officials around to guide and inform the cautious and the inquisitive.

Remember to take along binoculars, cameras and notebooks to record sightings of rare animals and birds. There are many excellent books that deal with our flora and fauna, and having these to hand after a lucky sighting makes for endless discussion. Our parks and reserves definitely are places to restore the soul of the nation and in this they admirably succeed.

WILDERNESS, BUSH OR MOUNTAIN CAMPS

These are considered the ultimate experience for the more adventurous and less fainthearted among us. If you're to enjoy yourself in these harsh environments – for example in the remoter parts of the country or in the mountainous regions accessible only on foot – you need some knowledge of the bush and a good level of physical fitness. Venues such as these almost always require special vehicles – not to mention special people!

Conditions in these camps can be severe, especially if they're situated in the desert or at high altitude, and in many cases there are no facilities at all. Visitors to the Richtersveld National Park in Southern Namibia, for instance, are expected to arrive in more than one 4x4 vehicle (you may need one to rescue the other) and be totally self-sufficient – you even have to supply your own water and firewood, and make sure you leave absolutely nothing behind.

Such an expedition requires an extensive range of equipment: steel cables, winches, high-lift jacks and many vehicle spare parts (ideally of the sort that can be replaced in the field). The amount of pre-planning is considerable.

BOOKING YOUR SPOT

Once you've chosen your venue, you need to secure your place. During the seasonal rush, you may need to pay a deposit: the amount will vary from a few per cent of the total cost to half the full payment up front. If you're a regular at a certain resort, book your next holiday a year in advance – don't wait until the last minute.

Find out about your chosen venue's preferred method of deposit and final payment, then check whether the payment has been received and that you have been sent all the relevant documentation.

This is essential when travelling far from home, and even more so when travelling beyond our national borders (when passports, and identification and other documents apply).

Once you've booked your time at the resort, try to reserve a specific site. This is not something you should take lightly. Some resorts may take the initiative and allocate a site on receipt of your deposit – check that the site you have been allocated is, in fact, suitable; if you have small children, you'll want to avoid a site too close to a river or pool, for example. Ask for the resort layout to be faxed or posted to you well in advance.

Most sites are numbered and you should receive this number in writing along with confirmation of your deposit payment. In some resorts, unfortunately, sites are allocated on a 'first come first served' basis.

If you are travelling out of the holiday season, a firm booking and deposit may be an unnecessary hindrance that ties you to a specific time and place. Weather changes, especially along the coast, may drive you to leave early, too. So don't automatically take the booking option – deposits are seldom refundable.

BEFORE YOU LEAVE HOME

A long journey by car is not half the ordeal it used to be in the past, but it still pays to get your car serviced and have all the crucial functions thoroughly checked; don't skimp on repairs. Roadside breakdowns are no fun, and anything you can do to avoid them is well worth the trouble. If you suspect a major fault, book the service well ahead of your departure date – and factor in more time for taking back the vehicle to have any 'settling down' problems sorted out as well.

Buy a good road map or two, which are available in a variety of formats from pocket-book guides to larger, more detailed, fold-out versions. These maps make navigating more fun, but they're also educational, showing many places of general interest to the traveller.

And knowing distances can be handy when you're estimating arrival times. I usually try to ignore the 'how long till we get there' question, but occasionally it's nice to be able to say, 'Oh, in about 45 minutes...' and be absolutely right.

Leaving an urban home unattended for even a short time is not wise these days, unless under the watchful eye of a reputable security company. Even then ... and this is no reflection on security companies! You may wish to organise a house-sitter instead. A person – or couple – known to you is one of the best options. If you have pets, find someone who is good with animals, who understands their habits and who is generally well disposed towards them. I say this because I know several people who 'have a thing about cats'. If you own one or more of these fascinating creatures, it would be unkind – to both parties – to leave them in the hands of someone who does not like them. Birds and fish can also be extremely temperamental (birds get lost and fish often just die) when left in uncaring hands.

That taken care of, it's time to get down to the nitty gritty. In these days of multi-vehicle families, we still try to pack everything we own into our largest vehicle. There may be sound logic behind this, but more and more people are opting to take both cars on holiday – and from here it's a short jump to going in convoy with several families and groups of friends. This can be great fun and provides for a wonderful feeling of security on the road. It's difficult to experience loneliness on a long, open stretch of the Great Karoo with three friends laughing hysterically on the back seat and another guffawing in your ear. Draw lots to drive the car full of kids, but remember, if you get the short straw you can always insist on swapping cars as time and stops allow.

If you wish to travel with a firearm, contact your local police station or the South African Gunowners Association (SAGA) to find out what is officially acceptable regarding storage and travel. You will be dealing with officialdom if anything goes wrong, so be sure to act within the law. The consequences of laxness can be dire, so as the licensed owner you need to be fully aware of your responsibility and take the necessary steps to ensure the security of your weapon. This does not mean that you have to carry it around with you the whole time.

Speak to the resort owner, who may provide a lock-up facility.

EQUIPMENT

The variety of outdoor equipment on offer can be bewildering. You may find yourself amazed by how little you can get away with, but you may be equally amazed to find how little you are prepared to do without. Your levels of enjoyment will be determined largely by your tolerances, and this doesn't apply only to campers, who live 'closer to the edge' in their tents.

Although it is possible to survive in the wilderness with very little, this is not the aim of the average holidaymaker. Everyone wants to have a good time, and the best way to do this is to have a clear idea of what sort of holiday you're after and then arrange things accordingly. If you intend staying in a tent, weight is unlikely to be a problem, but you will have to make a number of decisions and choices regarding the equipment itself.

If you decide to go caravanning, however, simply buy a caravan with everything you need built in. Your choices now will be governed by what vehicle you have and how many people will be accommodated, their ages and how many extras are necessary. Caravans have many optional accessories such as tents, awnings and add-on rooms, and you should examine the aftermarket carefully. Hiring before you buy is the best option. And don't hire one on site and just sleep in it! Go for the whole experience by towing it to a nearby destination.

LEAVING THE RESORT

Most resorts allow till midday to vacate a site, which gives the present guests time to pack and the staff members time to do whatever cleaning or tidying may be necessary before the next ones arrive.

Before you leave, check that any last-minute arrangements can be handled at a time convenient to both parties. Inform your hosts of your intended time of departure the day before. National parks, for example, are usually open during daylight hours only. So check the opening and closing times before

you invite frustration and inconvenience (for you and your host alike) by attempting to leave too early or arriving too late.

BACK AT HOME

The time to check your caravan and equipment for wear and tear is at the end of a vacation when everything is fresh in your mind. Make a note of the things that need repair or replacement as and when you find them (keep a small dedicated notebook for this purpose) and attend to them immediately on your return (unless they can't wait any longer).

Collect and store spare parts (such as washers, keys for gas bottles, tent pegs and spare neon tubes) with major items so they don't get left behind. Take particular care of items that may be hard to find and keep extra ones just in case.

All repairs to boat engines, motorbikes, bicycles and other vehicles are also best done at home when there is enough time, readily available expertise and spare parts. Take particular care to check any spare parts that wear quickly or are perishable, such as fuel filters.

CHAPTER TWO

LIFE IN A CAR

South Africa is a relatively large country; the distances between towns are far greater than those in Europe. Tell people how many hours are spent sitting in a car on an average holiday trip (36 hours solid both ways between Johannesburg and Cape Town, plus the time spent driving around once you are there) and you'll surprise even those who have done the journey often but not bothered to add it all up.

But think about long-distance travel this way – time-wise, you are in a situation seldom achieved anywhere else, except perhaps on an aeroplane. Cosily ensconced in your vehicle, you will be immune to many of the annoying diversions you experience elsewhere. In most cars there is no phone to answer (unless you take along your 'cell') and no one to call you away to hang out the washing or help tidy up. So make the most of it.

READING THE ROAD

Long-distance travel is probably one of the reasons that speeding and the consequent death toll on our roads are among the highest in the world. Some years back, a visiting driving instructor from the UK was asked to identify what he saw as the most widespread faults in South African driving habits. Apart from the overly aggressive attitude, he noticed that many South Africans drive with their attention riveted almost solely on the road in front of them, restricting their vision to only a short distance ahead; they pay scant attention to what may be happening behind them or on either side. As a result, they allow fractions of a second for reaction time if faced with a vehicle that is out of control.

In Europe and the UK drivers are encouraged to 'read the road' much further ahead, and be more aware of what is happening around them. Their 'sphere of awareness' tends to be much greater. Develop an awareness of your 'sphere' and you may be surprised to discover how small it is. Make a conscious effort to enlarge it and driving will suddenly become a pleasure. No matter how badly other people may appear to be driving, you will have given yourself time to 'read' their behaviour and find the chances of becoming involved in an accident considerably reduced.

The problem of staying awake on a long journey should not be underestimated. If everyone else is asleep, the driver may suffer more from the effects of fatigue. Heat and watching broken white lines flash by can contribute to a fatal accident. So take turns to drive; this will help break the monotony of a long spell on the road.

IN-HOUSE ENTERTAINMENT

When confronted with a long journey, try to make it part of the holiday. But no matter how dramatic the landscape, you will still be faced with the inescapable fact that you are confined to the car.

Groups of young people travelling without their parents seldom experience boredom. They've temporarily escaped 'the establishment', so the mood is ebullient, the conversation full of fun and jokes and the enthusiasm abundant. Add a good music system and the car may become a miniature travelling rock concert.

While groups of mature adults may prefer to listen to the life experiences of others, conversations are unlikely to last several hours. Here, a good collection of tapes or CDs will provide more unbroken listening time than you will ever get at home.

The many new radio stations offer a wide variety of material on the air, and tuning in to these can give you a taste of the local culture. Some lead a rather tenuous existence and welcome interest from anyone, so if you do have a phone in your car, why not call in and make direct contact.

But have you ever noticed how when you switch on the radio, all conversation stops? You could leave the music at home and watch how conversation spontaneously fills in the gap. (You may wish to keep the radio/CD/tape player hidden under your seat in case things don't go according to plan...)

The playing of musical instruments seldom goes down well in a moving car. And in any case, expensive instruments do not travel well without special care and are best left safely at home.

Card games are easily played on the move and, provided no money changes hands, can last for hours. Word games can also be a source of much amusement. Small prizes (or fun forfeits) can be dished out to the person who finds the most words or who makes up the most imaginative ones, for example, and for finding the word that contains all the letters in a game such as 'Target' (where nine letters are arranged in a square, and one word contains all the letters).

Those of a more literary nature may decide that the time would be best spent buried in an exciting novel (as long as they are not behind the steering wheel), or reading a favourite magazine from cover to cover. Books on travel abound, and it is possible to find travel-related volumes on almost every topic, from flora and fauna to history or the best restaurants in the part of the country you're visiting. All of these will add to your knowledge and enjoyment of a particular area.

Another way in which to banish boredom (a state of mind that seems to affect children and teenagers more often than adults) is to discover the 'collector' in each of us. Each kilometre can then become a miniature voyage of discovery.

Even comparatively whimsical subjects can provide hours of fascination, especially for children. Insects (dead ones of all sorts of interesting shapes and sizes), leaves, feathers, pebbles, shells, tree bark and seed pods, post cards, brochures, stickers, key rings and souvenirs (such as spoons carrying place names) are all part of the endless variety that awaits you.

But a word of warning: once born, ardent young collectors can become almost obsessional, and after a while their new-found hobby may require a certain degree of parental management. Every radiator becomes a trap for a never-ending supply of dead insects, every

CROPPING PHOTOGRAPHS

■ Once you've had your photographic prints made, it's even more fun to crop them. To do this, use thin, plain cardboard (the inside of a cereal box will do) to make two L-shapes large enough to surround a photographic print. You will use these to block out the unwanted parts of the picture around the edges.
■ Decide on the best way to trim each one, then simply snip off the unwanted bits, keeping the cuts parallel to the edge. After a little experimentation you will be amazed at how much better your prints look. Another plus is that they will now be in many different sizes and shapes, which will add variety. You will also be able to fit more pictures on each page of your album.

roadside stop a pebble-fanciers paradise. You'll find that a stand of half-dead blue gums next to the road becomes the potential hunting ground for that elusive piece of bark of a particular colour. Do not be surprised if you are asked to stop the car and scrape a dead locust off the windscreen for spare parts because 'my one has a leg missing!'

On circular trips, the occasional live insect can also be fun. A harmless tok-tokkie beetle will spend hours walking all over your children as they turn their hands and arms over and over again to stop it from falling off and hurting itself. Let it go where you found it – if you let it go somewhere else, you may introduce an alien, and cross-pollinating biomes is not a good idea for novices.

Wind-driven toys are another hit, but don't stick them out of the window – this is a good way to lose the toy, not to mention an arm!

Photography is an absorbing and not-too-expensive hobby (to begin with). Taken more seriously it can end up demanding a high level of expertise, even with simple equipment.

With encouragement, this hobby can provide the family travel photographer with a lifelong challenge. Recording places and events is fun, as you stay on the lookout for that next great shot, while building a portfolio of holiday pictures that will be the envy of your friends.

Tapes of books and plays (talking/listening books) are perhaps the most profitable way to use travel time in a car, especially if you are travelling alone. There is a wide variety of materials available: literary works, travel and detective stories, plays – you can even learn another language. If you have small children, there are tapes of delightful stories, nursery rhymes and songs.

One word of warning: a Shakespearean drama is very absorbing listening and can easily take a few hours. You may wish to avoid interrupting a particularly riveting part of the plot by stopping, so remember to check the petrol gauge every time you zoom past a filling station!)

UNDER THE SUN

Sun screens are something no traveller should leave home without, and they come in many shapes, sizes and colours. The most effective version for front and rear windscreens is the fold-up variety covered with silver foil (they're often sold at busy city intersections). They deflect heat as well as light and seem to reduce the greenhouse effect considerably. The cheapest option is also the most vulnerable to disintegration – cut and folded sheets of white cardboard. These screens are opaque, so can only be used when the car is parked.

On the other hand, screens for side windows can be used when the car is in motion. Some of these screens may be made of fine net or darkened plastic sheets, and they attach to the glass with soft plastic suckers; others have springy wire loops that expand firmly into the door or window frame. Both types are effective, but the latter keeps out the view.

A good pair of sunglasses will provide relief from the glare and make driving less tiring, but they must offer at least 99 per cent UV protection. Children need them possibly even more than adults. Buying a pair that they approve of will ensure they take good care of them and wear them when necessary.

COMFORT ZONE

Almost every passenger falls asleep on long journeys, and it's as well to find ways to make the afternoon nap as comfortable as possible. Make use of blow-up neck supports or cushions. Safety seats for children are a wonderful invention; the models that tilt back far enough for baby to lie on its back are the best of the lot. What a pity they don't make them for adults! Blankets and pillows make great back supports and are handy to sit on – and for short adults or teenagers, they improve the view out of the window.

If you have a car with air conditioning and don't mind paying for the extra fuel, all well and good, but a popular substitute is the oscillating dashboard fan available at most accessory shops. This wonderful device plugs into the cigarette lighter and can be set to oscillate, or direct a steady flow of air. Many have more than one speed setting.

MAPS

Detailed maps will provide interesting topographical information about the passing countryside. Government survey departments sell topographical maps to the public, which are designated by scale: for example 1:50 000 or 1:250 000. The amount of detail on these maps is astounding, but because the country is not surveyed annually, certain areas may show out-of-date information on the major routes. The land masses will be the same, though; the contours of every rise or depression are shown in 100m increments.

If you are venturing off-road into the remoter parts of our land, do not leave without a map that covers the area you will be visiting. A good pair of lightweight binoculars will bring the detail on the horizon into sharp focus and a compass will point you in the right direction. Survey maps are the final word when it comes to finding your way.

CHAPTER THREE

TENTS

If you're even thinking of going camping, you must like the idea of living in a tent. The good news is that there is an enormous range of tents, and the number continues to grow; every year seems to bring some new innovation.

The right tent will provide adequate shelter from the elements, allow reasonable freedom of movement inside and still have enough space left over to store sleeping bags, clothing and supplies. It will be easy to pitch and not take up too much space in the car or trailer.

When packed in their bags, most of the larger tents can easily be carried by two people; the total weight of the poles is usually in the region of 40 to 50kg. The smallest and lightest tents could weigh as little as 3 or 4kg. Most modern tents have waterproof ground sheets that form part of the cabin – the 'water column', given in centimetres, refers to the theoretical depth water can safely reach before penetrating the living area.

Generally speaking, most tents today are made of some synthetic fibre, even though the design may be old, as in a cottage tent. Having said that, canvas is still used here and there and remains an efficient, if comparatively heavy, covering. In rain the canvas swells, behaving somewhat like a canvas waterbottle: the spaces between the fibres close and it becomes quite waterproof. In this state it weighs a great deal more than when you put it up, as you will notice if you try to take it down or move it around! It will also take much longer to dry out than will a tent made of nylon. If stored un-aired for any length of time, a canvas tent will become mouldy and smelly and will eventually rot.

On the positive side, it is much harder to set a canvas tent alight, and the heavier gauge materials trap more air and provide more insulation from the elements.

The main advantages of modern fabrics are that they're water repellent – if not waterproof – they're lightweight, and for their weight are also very strong. Because the actual fibre is synthetic it cannot absorb water, and consequently it is quick to dry. The lightness of the fabric enables the tent to be rolled up into a small space, which is a significant factor when you are travelling.

'PLAY' TENTS

The smallest tents on the market are play tents. Although they offer plenty of amusement during the day, it is not a good idea to allow young children sleep in them unattended during the night. Waking up in unfamiliar surroundings can be a frightening experience for a small child – they usually need to know that they are in close proximity to their parents all the time.

Brightly coloured and often festooned with well-known cartoon characters and pictures, most play tents weigh less than a kilogram and are well worth taking along – where they'll fulfill the role of a holiday-time Wendy house.

COTTAGE TENTS

Cottage tents, after all these years, remain a popular option, even though they have been superseded many times by more advanced designs. Their stark simplicity has an irresistible appeal and, in spite of their dated (or should that be 'retro'?) look, they remain an efficient form of shelter.

They are easy to pitch and take down, and the roof provides a perfect run-off angle for water. The larger cottage tents are tall enough for standing room, not only in the middle where you need it but also right along the full length. Their lack of large windows is offset by the fact that they can often be opened at both ends to allow maximum air flow, something that is difficult to find in more recent designs.

A drawback is that certain models – in the manufacturers' efforts to retain the appeal of yesteryear – still come with no sewn-in ground sheets, which is a problem in damp weather. Some don't even have plastic skirts, which could at least have been dug into the ground.

DOME TENTS

The most popular tent shape is the dome. It is the result of extensive research, and dome tent designers make the best of many modern materials such as carbon fibre and Ventex to produce ranges in all sizes. These materials make use of advanced technology to provide shelters of unparalleled resilience – in many cases they have a strength-to-weight ratio that can only be described as phenomenal. The dome shape is intentionally aerodynamic, and the stiffeners provide a good degree of flex; such tents can survive strong winds, even if these are accompanied by snow, hail and sleet. Many come with a built-in wind-deflector as part of the fly sheet, which, if correctly positioned, provides additional shelter and helps keep gusts away from the main opening.

Depending on whether the tent has been purpose-designed or is for general use, the weight of the different models can vary considerably.

The lightweight versions are designed for hikers who wish to carry them as night-time shelters (a 2m x 2m x 1,8m tent may weigh as little as 6kg).

But, contrary to the claims of certain manufacturers, the life span of these tents may be shortened by extended time in the sun.

If you find a tent that seems suitable, check if the material has been impregnated with an ultraviolet-resistant component and if it has been treated with a fire retardant (in any event, avoid cooking inside small tents unless it's an emergency). Thin fabric catches fire easily, burns at a high temperature and incinerates in seconds rather than minutes. Rather cook in the shelter of the wind deflector, or at least try to remain outside the tent throughout the cooking procedure.

The larger dome tents provide a lot more comfort than do the smaller ones, although this depends on where you will be taking them. The standing room in a larger tent will be more convenient when getting dressed, and it will also provide a larger air space for the time you spend inside. In hot conditions this is a must. But if you are camping at high altitude you may value closer confines, as the temperature inside will be much easier to control. Too small a tent can induce mild claustrophobia during prolonged spells of inclement weather. You may also notice heavy condensation accumulating on the walls, and the tent will only remain comfortable for a few hours at a time.

If you want to pitch your tent for several days at one stretch, you will need one made from a fairly heavy material. The heaviest but most resilient fabric is similar to that used for army tents and seems to come only in shades of buff green. These tents are several times heavier than the hiking version, and nearly twice as expensive. They are also much more difficult to set alight, so cooking inside them is less of a danger. The four-person 2m x 2m x 1,8m version weighs about 20kg, and if unabused it should last a lifetime.

An outer fly sheet, usually made of heavier gauge material, will keep direct sunlight off the cabin and will provide an important air space between the two. If it has a veranda, this can provide momentary shelter if you are unlocking or unpacking in the rain; it will also provide shade on cloudless days. The fly sheet can be removed, but is best left on to protect what's underneath. If you use the tent for shelter during the day, the temperature inside with the fly sheet on will be several degrees lower than with it off.

Fine gauge mesh on all openings is a must-have, as mosquitoes and their friends can squeeze through the smallest of cracks.

FRAME TENTS

If you and your family intend staying in one place for any length of time, a frame tent is the way to go. These tents do take slightly longer to erect, but once up they afford a high level of comfort and convenience. The smallest of these will have a single room, but the largest may have up to three separate rooms and a communal area that can be used for dining or games during spells of bad weather.

Frame tents can have numerous components, so when you pitch yours for the first time, keep the instruction sheet handy to see what goes where. The frame is erected first – it is made of light aluminium poles that connect by simply sliding into each other. The joints lock together with an ingenious little device that produces a sharp click. It's a good idea to have some of these devices spare, as this is what holds everything together. The ends of these poles can be sharp when new, and could give you a nasty cut when you're trying to fit them into each other. The tent frames of better models have telescopic adjustable legs – a great help. Ordinary garden gloves will protect your hands.

With the frame up, all that remains will be to put on the covering and hammer in the pegs. There is no need to over-tension guy ropes, as they will do their job as long as they are firmly connected at both ends. To ensure a good shape to your tent, make sure that all opposing ropes pull evenly against each other.

The larger frame tents may not have an integral waterproof ground sheet, but even if they do, you will still need one under it that supports the entire floor area and allows the passage of air. Unlike the sheet that forms the floor of your tent, the best ground sheets resemble multi-layered shade cloth. Many resort owners insist on these, as their sites are less likely to be denuded of grass. Apart from providing a softer surface to walk on, they also save the floor of your tent from wear by keeping it off the ground. If you ever have to pitch your tent on a hard surface, you will be glad you've got one of these.

OTHER TYPES OF TENTS

If you intend travelling in a large vehicle such as a Kombi, you may wish to try a tent that fits snugly over the vehicle , extending its interior by several square metres. It works somewhat like a carport, and you can still drive the Kombi away – the inside door of the tent matches that of the vehicle, which allows access between the two without them being attached.

For school groups or sports tours of 20 people or more, look in the army surplus stores. The tents you'll find there are very big, and although they are sometimes used by campers they're more suited to caterers who hold large functions. They are sturdy but also very heavy, and require many strong hands to put them up and take them down. Such tents are usually associated with school outings, outer-fringe religious group gatherings and soldier-of-fortune reunion weekends.

Because of their size such tents tend to catch a lot of wind, and are difficult – if not impossible – to control in a squall.

Car-top tents are all the rage with the 4x4 fraternity. They are small compared to other tents, but then they are only ever meant to be slept in – the vehicle is used as storage space. They have several advantages. At the end of each day they provide their travel-weary owners with a perfectly flat platform on which to rest – although horizontal only comes if such a parking place can be found.

Exit and entry are by ladder, which means that the occupants are kept safe from ground-dwelling insects and prowling animals. And it can rain all night and you should remain bone dry – the nearest ground water will be a shade under two full metres below you. These tents attach directly onto your roof rack, so no pegs or ropes are necessary.

PEGS, ZIPS AND SPARES

For normal grassed stands, the best pegs are made from spring steel and the density of the earth provides the friction that determines the peg's holding capacity. Design-wise, the pegs shaped like a 'V' with an open circle attached to one end have the best ground-holding capacity and are used mainly on the guy ropes of larger tents. Simply hammer them into the earth so that the spring pushes down onto the ground, which in turn prevents the rope from slipping off should it work loose. To pull it out again, hook another peg around the bend in the 'V' and give a good tug. The distance from peg to tent should be about a metre.

You will need heavy-duty pegs if you are expecting to pitch your tent on very hard ground (it can still have grass on top). They should be made from high-tensile steel, be about 25cm long and 12mm in diameter and have straight shafts to absorb the serious hammering you are going to give them. Heavy-duty pegs have been bent into a hook at one end and sharpened at the other. To get them into the ground at a slight angle away from the tent you will need a 1kg hammer; the soft rubber one usually supplied with the tent is too light for the task. All things being equal, straight pegs do not have the same holding capacity as the V-shaped ones and are usually just used to keep down the sides of the cabin.

When you're buying a tent, don't forget the crucial element of doors and windows. Their zips should be strong and made from some non-corrosive metal such as brass. Nylon zips are very strong and can usually be trusted, but if you are shown something that looks like ordinary plastic, give it a miss. Each zip should have two robust travellers, which should have holes large enough to take a small lock should you need to leave your possessions unattended for any length of time.

Your repair kit should include spare eyelets (these are inexpensive and come in packets with a handy tool),

> ## STORAGE
>
> Once home, store your tent in a moisture-free environment. Treat it as you would a winter blanket: take it out to air every now and then. Micro-organisms do not like ultraviolet rays and sunlight will keep the fabric free of fungi and prevent it from smelling like a tent!

rope and a box of patches with the right adhesive. If you have bought a new tent, you may need to have it waterproofed. You can do this yourself with a can of resealing compound, which comes in a tin or aerosol can. Waterproofing wax is a good standby and is available in tins as light as 180g.

CHAPTER FOUR

TRAILERS

As your collection of equipment or – more likely – the collection of people you take with you on holiday starts to grow, everything that cannot or will not fit into or onto your car is going to have to go somewhere. The best place for it all is a trailer.

With a trailer you can take a lot more luggage – easily up to half the weight of your car – with very little fall-off in performance. With the extra weight behind you will need to start applying the brakes sooner, but there should be no restriction on your top speed, provided, of course, that you stay within the legal limit.

Because of its relatively low profile and the fact that it has a tendency to follow in the slip-stream of the tow-vehicle, a trailer is not much affected by cross-winds or headwinds.

Seen from a distance, the smaller trailers may seem too small to make any difference, giving the impression of a suitcase on wheels rather than meaningful packing space. Close-up, however, you will be surprised at how big they are. Essentially a large, straight-sided metal box with no inner protuberances, strange contours or bulges, the nature of the space is very different to that of the average car boot – and much easier to pack.

Most trailers consist of a sheet-metal box and lid, attached to a frame or chassis made from square-sectioned metal tubing. Some manufacturers offer a 'box' constructed out of fibreglass, which is light, strong and aerodynamically shaped with racy curves. This does not provide nearly as much packing space as the squarer models, but for the more image-conscious traveller the aesthetic body styling does produce an extravagant, upmarket look.

These trailers are among the few models that come in a variety of colours. The metal parts of the more expensive models may be galvanised before being painted or epoxy coated, depending on the resilience required of the finish. The frame and the undersides of all the components such as mudguards are usually painted with a thick rubberised coating, which causes stones and other sharp objects to bounce off.

Trailers are fitted with the rear lights, brake lights and indicators required of any vehicle, and these are usually enclosed in the body work. This is done to protect them from damage during reversing. All trailers have a height-adjustable foot behind the tow-hitch, which supports the front of the trailer and keeps it level once it has been detached from the vehicle. The heaviest trailers have a jockey wheel at the end of the foot, which allows the front end to be moved without having to be lifted off the ground.

NOSE CONES

As an optional extra, some trailer manufacturers offer a nose cone. This smaller compartment fits on top of the triangular section of the chassis between the tow-hitch and the leading edge of the luggage compartment. The lid hinges at the back and locks at the front. Because of its size it is very handy for storing things that you might need often. One trailer model comes with a nose-cone shape that does not open from above but is, in fact, an extension of the interior. This addition is particularly handy when long objects such as tent poles or masts need to be accommodated.

In some rural areas these trailers are popular alternatives to the funeral hearse – they're long enough to accommodate a coffin!

Although a nose cone does make the trailer look less boxy, it offers very little advantage from an aerodynamic point of view.

WHEELS

The wheels of ordinary luggage trailers are a lot smaller than those of the average motor car, meaning that they do more revolutions at the same speed. But a trailer used only occasionaly will not go through many sets of tyres. For practical purposes, some of the heavy-duty

GETTING CAUGHT IN A SPIRAL

■ In reversing a trailer or caravan into a given space, there are two things to remember: cars reverse in circles; trailers and caravans in spirals. If you hold your car's steering wheel at a constant angle, the vehicle will proceed along the circumference of a wide circle, the constant curve making it easy to anticipate the path of the car. When you reverse a trailer, however, anything even fractionally either side of a dead straight line will send the trailer off on an ever-decreasing spiral in the opposite direction. The trailer is extremely sensitive to deviation, and the greater the increment the more acute the spiral. Driving a car and trailer backwards in a dead-straight line may be possible only by accident, but with very small turns of the wheel, you will find, nevertheless, that you can control the path of the trailer.

■ To begin with, keep the car and trailer as close to a dead-straight line as possible. Practice reversing in an empty parking lot. Do not reverse quickly. 'Funeral march' your trailer back bit by bit.

■ Control the diameter of the car's turning circle and you will control the path of the trailer. The greater the angle of the car's front wheels, the smaller the turning circle.

■ Having started on a constant curve, the car will always try to overtake the inside wheel of the trailer. This is the start of the spiral. Unless the car's path is adjusted, the trailer spirals in around the path of the inside wheel. Correct this by steering in the opposite direction. This will serve to straighten the path of the trailer. Only experimentation will tell you how much to turn the wheel.

■ Every spiral starts with a long, slow curve. As long as you never allow the trailer to get into the tight 'inner reaches' of the spiral, it will continue to move backwards in a series of long, slow curves.

- Once you've gauged the sensitivity of your steering, it is quite possible to steer the trailer anywhere you want it.

Some further points to ponder

- A motor car has four wheels arranged in two parallel lines. The distances between these lines cannot change. When you set the front wheels at an angle and reverse the car, it goes backwards in the arc of a perfect circle.
- A trailer tends to 'pivot' on the inside, having a multiplier effect on the curve it follows. It does this in an ever-decreasing circle, the radius of which gets smaller.

safari trailers carry the same size wheel and tyre as the tow-vehicle.

Spare wheels are usually fixed under the chassis near the back, but on a safari or off-road trailer this would reduce clearance so they are fixed either to the side of the trailer or to the lid. Many are tied onto the roof-rack, which makes them vulnerable to theft; most owners simply store them inside the trailer. If this is not practical, then some sort of lock-up device is called for.

Off-roaders tend to choose items that have many uses, so some carry a hefty length of chain and a padlock. With the spare wheel locked inside, you can chain the trailer and all its contents to a tall tree. A good, lightweight alternative to carrying a spare wheel is to keep an aerosol can of puncture sealant handy, although, depending on the size of the tyre, you might need a big one!

SUSPENSION

Suspension on any trailer is basic by modern standards and usually consists of leaf springs of various carrying capacities; the strength of the suspension is in direct proportion to the size of the load.

Although most safari or off-road trailers keep to two-wheel configurations, the larger luggage trailers often go to four. This makes for better directional stability and provides better support for the chassis, as the ends of the springs on either side are further apart.

MUDGUARDS

Mudguards stop stones from flying up and hitting any following vehicles, but on the more robust trailers they also double-up as steps and supports for jerry cans of fuel or water. The mudguards on most trailers are not designed to carry much weight, and habitual misuse of them will produce cracks along the top edges and provide a foothold for the onset of rust.

If you'll be travelling in convoy over untarred roads or patches of gravel near roadworks, know that rocks and stones thrown up by the wheels of speeding vehicles can achieve surprisingly high velocities and be extremely dangerous. Mudflaps have a dampening effect on their trajectory and help keep them close to the ground.

LUGGAGE RACKS

For the long-distance traveller or accessory-hungry holidaymaker, a luggage rack that fits onto the trailer's lid may be the ideal place to store canoes, bicycles, tents, tables or more camping gear. If the rack is strong enough and of the right dimensions, you will be able to find a tent that fits it, so the whole entourage can end up sleeping 'airborne' on top of the vehicle. One such tent on the market even has extensions that form a side-tent. A word of caution at this stage: the more you put on the lid of the trailer the heavier it will become. Gas-assisted lifters may help, but unaided access to the luggage inside may still be difficult – if not impossible – for certain members of the party.

TRAILER VARIATIONS

The top-of-the-range safari trailer is truly the 'ultimate' outdoor vehicle. Hugely impressive, it exists in a rarefied atmosphere all its own. Priced accordingly, it will be made from stainless steel, have a built-in bar (stock it yourself), insulated nose cone, shock absorbers, fridge or cooler box, fully equipped kitchen with gas stove, water and fuel tanks (with external fitted taps), gas struts on the lid, a generator, storage bins over the wheel housings, spare wheel, corner stabilisers and a full range of roof-top tents that can sleep up to six adults.

The axle 'track' will be made to match that of the towing vehicle.

Custom modifications, within reason, may be included at little or no extra charge. If this isn't enough, you may choose from a wide range of optional extras, which may include crockery/cutlery sets, secondary battery systems and lights, toolboxes and over-run braking.

Several models of these vehicles exist, and can handle the worst terrain in Africa.

Other useful variations on luggage trailers are tailgates that flap down so that heavier objects need only be lifted to floor level when loading. They also make the use of ramps much easier. Extra-high sides with large rear doors allow taller objects, such as cupboards and boxes, to be transported in a secure environment, while mobile kennels fitted with gauze-covered windows permit animals to travel in relative comfort.

There's even a trailer that has a raiseable roof and fabric walls with windows to accommodate couples who don't mind sleeping very close together on a sort of mobile double bed. This option would be more comfortable than a tent and, depending on whether or not you choose the collapsible tent model, it requires little effort to put up.

CHAPTER FIVE

CARAVANS

Buying a caravan is an exciting prospect, but it isn't something that should be taken lightly. A new one will be a sizable investment, so make sure that you are buying the right make and model. A good second-hand one may cost less at first, but unless you're sure it is quite sound, you may be in for another – large – bill later. With caravans, older usually means heavier and more cumbersome, although some of the more classic designs still have a unique charm if you are going on a nostalgia trip. Take your time looking and do not be in a hurry to close a deal (unless it's a genuine bargain!). Only make the final decision once you have considered all the options.

The biggest decision, of course, is whether or not you actually want to buy one at all. If you're at all unsure, reread chapter three about tents.

Once you've decided that you definitely do want to buy a caravan, check that your car is capable of towing one! If you have a car that meets the needs of a young family, the chances are excellent that you will find dozens of caravans that it can safely tow. But do make sure, just to be on the safe side. Most people buy a caravan to suit their car, although the opposite would not be too rare an occurrence.

There are many features that give caravans their unique appeal, but the main one is that all essential items are permanently in one place. The convenience and sheer comfort of having everything in a single, purpose-built package should never be underestimated. Depending on the size of the party, beds can often be left made-up and clothing and the galley (kitchen) cupboards can be left packed the way you like them. Your caravan is literally a holiday house on wheels – perhaps it's even better than a holiday home, as you have the choice of varying your destinations.

The set-up time for a caravan without its tent is negligible. Disconnect the tow-hitch from the car and make minor adjustments to the positioning (not always necessary). Then wind down the corner steadies to level it, connect or turn on the power supply – and sit back and relax. The total time taken can be mere minutes. For the travel-weary tourist this is what makes owning a caravan really worthwhile! Your car is free for shopping trips, sightseeing or excursions into town, and you find yourself literally home away from home.

Your choice of caravan type will depend on your holidaying habits. Many overnight stops would mean a lot of pitching and packing away of tents and other equipment; although almost all caravans have a tent, you may decide not to pitch it and use the caravan itself as the main source of accommodation.

Bear in mind that a small caravan is designed to carry about 200kg of extra weight, and this should not be exceeded. So you'll need to carefully monitor how much weight you take with you. The size of caravan you choose will be governed largely by the interior layout and its other features. In order to appeal to as wide a market as possible, all caravans are designed to be used in a number of ways, and their most-popular sleeping or seating configurations depend on the habits of the occupants. Although even the smallest caravans appear large if you are used to towing a trailer, it is more their shape and overall size that makes them seem formidable. You may be surprised to find that the smaller caravans weigh about 590kg empty; this is roughly the weight of a full trailer.

THE TWO-BERTH CARAVAN

Caravans are categorised by the number of berths (beds) they provide without the use of extensions such as tents, and the smallest of these is a two-berth. They are the cheapest caravans on the market, are built with couples in mind and are small, light and easy to handle.

The two-berth does not offer much in the way of layout versatility, however; the only real option is the possible conversion of the double bed into a four-seater dinette. A big plus is the extreme lightness of this diminutive caravan, which means it can be towed by a small car or bakkie in the 1300cc class. Two-berth layouts are, logically, extremely popular with those who require little space, but as they have limited general appeal there are not a great many makes from which to choose.

The interior of a two-berth will not be elaborate. A typical layout would consist of a dinette that can convert into a double bed (or the other way round, depending on how you look at it), and a small galley housing, perhaps, a two-burner gas stove with a small refrigerator underneath and a washing-up basin on one side. Packing space is provided in cupboards and in bins under the seats. Small but ample shelving and a shower cubicle or cupboard space opposite the galley would complete the arrangement.

Ventilation is important in such a small space, and a 'pop top' roof will provide a good cross-flow of air while giving taller members of the party much-appreciated headroom. In an effort to enlarge all available space, the entire back wall of the Caravette 2 folds out and is supported on two aluminium legs. A three-sided tent rolls down to provide extra living space, which can easily accommodate two more people or become a dining area. One wall of the tent provides the missing door. A possible minus point here is that unless the back is folded out, there is no point of entry.

The Sprite Scout, another two-berth, not only has a normal door but a shower/toilet cubicle as well.

THE FOUR- TO SIX-BERTH CARAVAN

The next size up is the four- to six-berth range. This is the most popular category and can accommodate a family and one or two friends with ease.

Some couples also choose to travel in a four-berth. Many four-berths are still small as caravans go (the old Sprite Sprint is a good example); they're only marginally bigger than their two-berth cousins and weigh almost the same. The

Sprite has a layout comprising a double bed at the rear and a two-seater dinette in front, with a galley and cupboard space separating the two. Because as a couple you will be catering for only two people, the weight factor will remain low, but the big advantage is that set-up time will be reduced to an absolute minimum. Tents and patios are usually optional, and if you choose not to buy them, this will reduce weight still further. A four-berth used by two people is caravanning at its wonderfully convenient best.

Older four-berth models tend to have all the sleeping areas convertible into seating of one sort or another, but the modern vans do not. People seldom crowd inside a caravan to eat when there is so much fresh air and scenery about. If the weather turns foul, many outdoor enthusiasts find that their tolerance levels drop fast, and instead of getting all steamed up inside, they simply find the nearest restaurant and eat out. (If you notice the weather deteriorating, be sure to leave early, as the foul-weather queues at steakhouses and fast-food outlets can sometimes make the steamy galley a better option!) A four-berth galley is designed with catering rather than just cooking in mind, and the air space inside is noticeably larger. Many have a locker in which to house a microwave oven – microwaves generate a lot less heat, apart from cooking food more quickly.

PERSONAL SPACE

When you're choosing a caravan, ask yourself whether there is enough 'personal space' to make owning it a pleasant experience, even though you will tend not to spend a lot of time inside. A caravan can be a cosy haven during a rainstorm and a wonderful place to have a good read, but it can also be positively claustrophobic. If the space affects you adversely in any way, you will not want to spend time there, and this will limit the pleasure you get out of your vacation.

STORAGE SPACE

Weight and space will dictate what you take with you on your holiday and what you leave behind. So before you buy your caravan, have a good, hard look at the amount of cupboard and other types of space, under-bed bins, galley cupboards etc., and assess whether it will accommodate you with minimal sacrifices. You are unlikely to find something that is totally unsuitable, as most manufacturers use space extremely well. But all models are not exactly the same, and you may find that certain storage configurations suit you much better than do others. This is not necessarily something that you can measure with a tape and a calculator – you may just like one more than another, and it is important that you do.

COLOUR

Colour is vitally important in our lives, and scientists discovered some time ago that colours really do affect our moods. Architects and designers take great care when selecting the interior colours for large and expensive high-rise buildings, for example. They are aware that the choices they make will affect productivity, so they try to make this effect a positive one.

Generally speaking, colours that are too dominant become overbearing and are difficult to live with for any length of time. Likewise with patterns on curtains, bed linen, interior trim, work surfaces, upholstery coverings and a whole host of other items. In an effort to please as many people as possible, manufacturers tend to go for neutral colours, which hopefully do not intrude or have any negative effects (the aim is to have a slight edge in terms of creating a positive and enticing atmosphere).

WINDOWS

Windows are even more important in caravans than they are in your home, as they provide ventilation for a much smaller interior. Modern caravan windows are made from a single piece of moulded acrylic with hinges, arms and handles attached. They close from the outside, sealing the entire window aperture, and are usually tinted in pastel shades. The handles turn-to-lock inside, and adjustable arms allow you to set the angle at which you want to leave them open.

Older windows were made of shatterproof glass, and although they presented a clearer picture of what was going on outside, they were also heavier and more complicated to make. If you are buying second-hand, watch out for cracks; minor cracks around the fittings are usually nothing to worry about, but large ones may mean that a point of attachment is about to go.

Unless your caravan is air-conditioned, windows will be your main means of lowering the inside temperature, so the bigger the better. Not all windows will open, but those that do need to have mosquito netting (this is something you may have to add yourself). Large front and back windows are the most important of all, as the driver can use the rear-view mirror of the car to look through them onto the road behind. Many caravanners do not realise this and drive with the curtains closed. If you see someone driving in this way, please do your civic duty and enlighten them; it improves safety on the roads.

POWER

Most caravans have two main sources of power: gas and electricity. The latter comes from a normal 220-volt power point via an extension lead that is supplied with the caravan. Power is channelled via a small mains box, which is essentially a distribution board with trip switches and a transformer. When it is plugged in and switched on it automatically recharges the battery, which provides the 12-volt power source for the interior lights and other 12-volt appliances such as shavers. Although the lighting will be 12 volt, there are usually one or more power points that provide 220 volts in the form of a normal household plug and switch. Check that there are enough of these, should you wish to take your toaster, TV, kettle, video recorder, food mixer or food processor along. It will become a nuisance if you have to keep plugging in and unplugging appliances. It shouldn't be too difficult or expensive to have more plugs fitted.

All caravans must have a fire extinguisher. And it must be where you can get your hands on it in a hurry. The device that keeps it in place needs to be strong but must be able to be opened without delay. Everyone must know where it is, so buy one that comes with a holder that can be bolted or screwed onto a bulkhead. Position it near the door so that in the event of a fire you do not need to enter the burning caravan to get your hands on it. It must never be left lying loose or it will end up being packed away and not available when you need it most. Later-model caravans will usually have a small recess to house this vital device.

THE GALLEY

The galley can become a place of concentrated activity and it needs to be a space that works – preparing food in one that does is always a pleasure. All caravans have a galley or kitchen area, although I have seen a recent model that does not have a cooker of any sort. This may sound impractical to most of us, but if it's to be used by weekenders who only ever braai, a stove might be an unnecessary expense. In most caravan models, however, there is a gas stove with at least two burners. Some models include a place for a microwave, which means you can choose the make and model – and you may decide to bring along the one from home instead of owning two. In the larger caravan models, though, it is not unusual to find a microwave and gas cooker already installed. Eye-level microwaves are more popular than conventional ovens, as the amount of heat generated by the latter is keenly felt inside a caravan.

Galley layouts vary greatly. The more sophisticated layouts focus on a central point: all the items are as close to this as possible, and the size of the remaining work surfaces are determined by the size and placement of the cooker and washing-up area.

Hobs, like almost everything else to do with caravanning, are available in many shapes and sizes. How many burners you need depends on the cooking and eating habits of the family. Many are built on a pressed stainless-steel plate, which should be easy to clean and able to cope with any wear and tear. Some have a rather industrial feel, which does not endear them to everyone, while others have enamel or other finishes that are as hardwearing yet brighten up the interior with a subtle touch of colour.

Many four-burner hobs are square, which means you can change the position of the switch panels simply by turning the hob through angles of 90°. If there are small children about, position the switches along the inside edge where they will be less noticeable and away from little hands.

If you're going to be catering for a large party where most of the cooking will be done indoors, consider buying an additional free-standing gas stove and a second refrigerator. Both these items will live outside in the tent area, which copes easily with the heat given off by a full-size stove. If this sounds a bit excessive, imagine trying to cook three meals a day for 15 people on a four-burner hob. A 140-litre refrigerator class will be big enough – as long as you already have another one like it inside. Take care with extra gas leads and wiring so that they're not a hazard to the increased traffic. Refrigerators are usually designed to run off either gas or electricity, and having both options is wonderfully convenient.

For extra storage in the galley, shelving is the best option, and a good set of aluminium shelves will take up the least floor space and weigh very little. Food items need to be easy to get to, and if you can take everything in at a glance it makes the estimated time of consumption much easier to calculate. Strong cardboard boxes, as long as they are not too large, are wonderful as you can just dump them before you go home (although if they are of the sort that have been designed to last – like apple boxes – their lightness and strength may make you want to hang on to them a while longer). They make great temporary waste bins when lined with a black bag, and giving everyone a box in which to keep their 'junk' does wonders for keeping the tent tidy.

L-shaped galleys are becoming more popular: the foot of the 'L' doubles as a room divider, isolating the main cooking area, and it also provides privacy in what becomes a small bedroom. This gives a refreshingly new look to the whole interior, creating an attractive kitchen area that is as inviting as it is practical.

VENTILATION

Fortunately, the trend in South Africa is to have lots. Most modern caravan designers make superb use of one of the greatest inventions in caravanning. The 'pop-top' roof has increased in size and sophistication and today the evolution can be considered just about complete. In many models almost the entire roof area lifts up on gas-assisted struts.

Positive locking mechanisms, which can be operated from the inside, keep it in place – either up or down. When up, the headroom inside is increased to about 2m, and when down it provides a significantly lowered profile for towing.

SLEEPING ARRANGEMENTS

Beds that do not convert into seating provide a more stable sleeping platform, as the mattresses do not have the divisions required for seating. They also provide more storage space underneath the mattress, as they don't need the floor space necessary in a dinette.

Modern caravan designers, recognising the need for privacy, have included sliding partitions that seal off the main sleeping area. Some even go so far as to have two separate rooms, each with its own door leading outside (this will, of course, affect the interior traffic).

Bedside pedestals always seem like a good idea, even though they can often be quite small. A simpler option is achieved when the bed is positioned in one corner and a low shelf runs the length of the bed along the opposite side. This provides one large space rather than two smaller ones, which will suit some but not others. Make sure that the distance from the top of the pedestal to the bed is short enough to keep everything within reach.

WATER

Running water is a standard feature in every caravan except the most Spartan, and over the years this has been provided for in a number of ways. If you are buying secondhand you may encounter systems such as a foot-operated pump, or a small eye-level tank that needs to be filled by hand and the water drawn out by gravity. These are both low-pressure systems by any standards, but so simple as to be almost totally trouble free. Another system uses a small electric pump that lifts water from a container outside the galley. Used water simply runs out under the caravan.

More sophisticated systems pump air into an underfloor tank, the pressure forcing the water out of the taps or shower. A remote-control switch activates the pumps, so that pressure is maintained while the tap is in use. A good hot-water system will have two tanks: a large one for storage, carrying 60 to 80 litres, and a smaller geyser that carries an easy-to-heat 20 litres. A pilot flame may have to be ignited by hand, but more sophisticated units have sensors that detect the gas flow and ignite the flame by pushing an interior switch to the 'on' position. Geysers should be switched off in the event of the caravan being unoccupied for a number of days.

AIR CONDITIONING

Because all the large caravans are electrified, it is quite possible to have air conditioning. This will add to the weight but there are some things in life that can't be measured in kilograms (or rands). Even among the macho 'I-can-take-it' fraternity, the searing temperatures of the country's interior continue to make this a popular option. Although most units are installed as a permanent fixture, good-quality portable models exist that can be shared between house and caravan, or between rooms when at home.

SHADE

Awnings or patios provide a surprising amount of shelter, and you should go for the best you can afford in this department as they will absorb some serious punishment from the sun. Lighter colours reflect more heat than do dark ones, and you will already know that the temperatures in the shade are many degrees lower than in the sun. By night they'll provide dew-protection for extended parties and expensive tow-vehicles.

Many caravans have places to attach a second awning – good as an extra outdoor-living area or a car shelter. Most tents have a built-in awning but the two items can be bought separately.

TENTS

Investigate all the options to find one that suits you. The basic unit is a frame tent, where the width extends along the full length of the caravan and the poles attach to the

THE PRE-TRIP CHECK

Never rush the pre-trip check list. Most caravans have a sticker inside the door or some equally prominent place that reads something like this:
- External electricity supply disconnected.
- Windows/roof vents closed, locked.
- Gas appliances off.
- Roof (low-profile models) down and locked.
- Gas bottle valves off.
- Corner steadies up.
- Coupling head safety-catch engaged.
- Jockey wheel stem up and locked.
- Safety-chain positioned behind wheel.
- 7-pin plug and road lights connected and checked.
- Caravan handbrake off.
- Caravan door locked and everything inside secure.
- Water tanks empty (unless you are planning on taking water with you). Depending on your planned water usage, it's better, when travelling, to keep the tanks either full or empty. A half-filled tank of water sloshing around can build up a fair momentum, which will induce sway when you least need it.

caravan wall. The canvas is led along the caravan profile with runners and will extend out some 2m or more. The roof will cover the entire frame, including the patio, and is attached to the poles with fabric or Velcro ties; the poles may also be slid into sleeves sewn into the roof along major seams. The panels that hang down from the frame are usually attached with zips, which can be removed individually so that the entire tent can become one large awning.

Many tents are still made with thick plastic skirts sewn all along the bottom edges, but to fulfil their function of keeping water out of the living area during wet spells and creepy crawlies out the rest of the time they need to be dug into shallow trenches – and I cannot see this being allowed on the pristine lawns that have taken many a caravan-park owner weeks or months to cultivate. To avoid a confrontation, fold them in to keep the plastic skirts out of the sun.

A large net ground sheet that covers the whole floor area, including the patio, is a must and will prevent sand and grit from getting onto the far more sensitive floor surfaces of your caravan.

The temperature inside the tent area is regulated by the natural flow of the air, which is in turn controlled by the size and positioning of the windows and doors.

Windows in any tent are basically large openings covered with mosquito netting, and here you might have to choose between the lesser of two evils. The tighter the weave of the net, the more efficient it is as an insect barrier, but the more it will restrict the air flow and the hotter your tent will be.

Mosquitoes can get through the tiniest of holes, and not all mesh is sufficiently tightly woven to keep them out. If in doubt, always go for the weave with the smallest openings. There are many other ways to keep cool and calm, but keeping 10 000 mosquitoes from eating you alive is more complicated.

GETTING ORGANISED

You will need to organise your outdoor living space to suit your daily activities. The greater the level of activity the more tidying up there is likely to be, and the idea is to keep this to a minimum.

If there is a beach or river nearby, you don't want sodden water nymphs dragging wet clothing, towels and sand into the caravan – so keep a water-filled foot basin just inside the door.

If the children are sleeping in the tent or if it's being used as a general living or dining area (more likely all three together), try to find a place for everything. Items like watches and jewellery should go inside the caravan, but if it's stuff that goes on and off all the time, it's best kept outside.

PACKING

Packing is generally a simple matter, but done really well it becomes an art. When packing a caravan and its tow-car, think of them as a single unit – once they're attached that is exactly what they will be. Both need to be well balanced, and having the right weight in the right places will ensure a safe and pleasant journey. When fully loaded, and that includes the occupants, the caravan should be slightly nose-down with the weight on the towbar between 60 and 80kg. Ask someone else to take your place in the driver's seat while you stand back to check the angle. Apart from placing undue strain on the rear suspension, too much weight on the back of the car will tend to lift the front wheels, reducing steerage and encouraging swaying. Cross-winds can play havoc in a situation like this, and unexpectedly strong gusts can have hazardous results. If you hit an unexpectedly hard bump, excessive weight on the towbar can also result in a cracked tow-hitch.

Inside your caravan, most of the heavy objects, such as tents, should be placed over the axles, with the exception of the main gas bottles, which live in the front storage area behind the towbar. Lighter things such as sleeping bags, blankets or clothing can be evenly distributed on either side. No weight should be placed right at the back of the caravan and everything should be secured so that it cannot slide around. Use soft items like sleeping bags to cushion more rigid ones like chairs or braai units. This helps to protect the interior trim of the caravan and stops things rattling, which can be very distracting for the driver.

SAFETY ON THE ROAD

THE VIEW AHEAD

It's difficult to give exact figures regarding the distances between yourself and the car in front of you – suffice it to say that they should be much greater than normal (about an extra 60–100 per cent). Much depends on the speed and density of the traffic and the condition of the road. Tight curves or an uneven road surface require much more care on the part of the driver, who needs to be thinking ahead so that any possible avoiding action can be taken. Sudden stops when towing at speed are all but impossible and should be avoided at all costs, if only because they usually create a bigger accident!

TRAFFIC

There is really no other way to say it: towing in heavy traffic is unpleasant and should be avoided if at all possible. No matter how slow your speed, difficult situations will continue to arise as belligerent, misguided motorists keep cutting in front of you, shortening the crucial following distance by making themselves the new car in front. Plan your travel times to avoid traffic if you possibly can.

MIRRORS AND STABILISER BARS

There are many things you can do to make towing a caravan easier, and the good news is that two of them can be bolted onto your car. One is a set of large rear-view mirrors and the other is a stabiliser bar. The purpose of the former is self-explanatory, and many motorists will have seen tow-cars wearing them – they greatly expand the driver's field of vision to include what is happening around and behind the caravan.

The mathematics needed to explain the action of stabiliser bars is a lot more complicated, but in essence what they do is to lock the car and caravan onto the same track with a device that bolts onto the towbar. This ingenious invention controls sideways movement (swaying) as well as any up-and-down movement (pitching) that may occur – the latter by cleverly transferring weight to the front wheels of the car. Different designs achieve this to varying degrees; one new design – the Trapezium – is so good that, apart from the actual weight, there is almost no sensation of towing at all. You can fit the Trapezium yourself – all you need do is drill a single hole and the rest just bolts together.

SUSPENSION

Special shock absorbers and other devices that attach into and onto the springs can beef-up the back suspension and allow the car to carry a heavier load on the back axles. Some shock absorbers can be adjusted for height, allowing the rear of the car to ride higher than usual in an effort to accommodate a heavier-than-normal load. An extra oil cooler can be fitted to help control the temperature of the oil, which will get hotter than normal because of the increased friction.

GEAR RATIOS

Some vehicles have sophisticated automatic gearboxes with adjustable gear ratios that are 'tweaked' to cope with the increased load. This is going a bit far for the average motorist, although it does depend on how seriously you take the towing ability of your car. Well-chosen accessories can do much to enhance the driving or towing experience, but competition is fierce and caution is urged. Quality of workmanship, not to mention reputation, is very important.

SPEED

No matter how good your driving habits, no one is immune to equipment failures such as tyre blow-outs or axle failures, to quote but two common examples. There is one aggravating factor in all accidents, however, and that is speed.

The speed at which you tow your caravan depends on the size of the caravan and the strength of the tow-vehicle, but a safe speed would be between 90kph and 110kph.

Gathering speed on a steep downhill is often the cause of the classic caravan accident. After crawling up a steep hill, the temptation is to go down the other side at breakneck speed in order to build up enough momentum to take you as far up the following hill as possible. This is one of the most dangerous things you can do with a caravan, and once you've lost control you will find it almost impossible to regain. A jack-knife accident occurs when you discover that you're going too fast. You push the brake pedal, but the caravan (usually with no brakes of its own) has such momentum that it tries to overtake the car by pushing the back of the car out of the way. The car and caravan, at high speed, fold up like a jackknife. The way to save the situation is to accelerate so that the car starts pulling the caravan once more, but if you are already going dangerously fast this may only compound the problem.

CAR SPEED AT MAXIMUM TORQUE

'92 Toyota Cressida 2,4l Gl
1st gear 24kph
2nd gear 42kph
3rd gear 62kph
4th gear 85kph
Top gear 100kph

'92 Opel Rekord 200i CIS
1st gear 28kph
2nd gear 52kph
3rd gear 82kph
4th gear 117kph
Top gear 140kph

'94 Mazda B2600 DC
1st gear 18kph
2nd gear 28kph
3rd gear 47kph
4th gear 76kph
Top gear 87kph

(*Figures courtesy of *Car* Magazine.)

The best way to handle hills is not to rush down them as fast as you can. To grasp this fully, take a look at the workings of your car. Every car's engine has a speed (measured in rpm) that produces the most power (maximum torque) in each gear, and every motorist towing a caravan should memorise these figures for his or her car (see *Car Magazine's* road tests). Too slow and you strain the engine, too high and you waste fuel. Do not allow the rpm to wander too far from maximum torque – you may get there 15 minutes later but the life of your engine, not to mention your own, will be extended. This information is particularly useful when climbing hills and mountain passes.

When you begin to descend a hill, maintain a constant speed, somewhat slower than at maximum torque, from the crest to about four-fifths of the way down the hill. (If it is a very steep hill, run under compression: in gear – top or third – but with your foot off the accelerator.) Some time just before the road levels out is the time to start accelerating (knowing the exact moment requires some judgement). Being on a downhill, the car should gather momentum quickly, and you should engage

WIND AND THE ART OF TOWING

Wind is the enemy of any caravanner, and towing into a strong headwind is one of the most frustrating features of any trip. Your fuel consumption soars and your speed drops. There is also something about strong wind that can make people irritable and edgy. Watch out for sharp curves, as a strong wind can become treacherous and hit you from unexpected angles. Narrow roads or steep passes are the worst places to encounter cross-winds, as in both cases there is little margin for error. Although seldom the sole cause of an accident, erratic cross-wind can be as nerve-wracking for oncoming traffic as they are for the driver. If conditions start looking extreme, find an alternative route, which can save time and frustration.

Unfortunately, towing into a following wind is also not a pleasure; your steering may suddenly feel light as you get an extra push from behind. The force of the wind (along the False Bay coastline it can reach 80kph) pushes the caravan forward and down onto the towbar, taking weight off the front wheels of the car. This will not be dangerous in itself, but on a bumpy stretch of gravel road, where the bouncing wheels are not making full contact with the ground anyway, it can make for very uneasy going. To give the wind its due, it can help a great deal as you're going up a hill – so if this ever happens to you, be sure to savour the moment.

the start of the uphill section with the engine running a little over maximum torque in top gear. At this stage you will have all the momentum you are ever going to get from your car at a safe speed.

As the hill gets steeper you will feel the car slow down. Run at maximum torque for as long as you can, but change down, sooner rather than later, as you feel the power fading. You will now find your engine running at just over maximum torque again, but in a lower gear. If it's a steep hill, you may even have to go down as far as second, but as you reach the top of the hill, the car will start to accelerate once more. Do not change until you are comfortably in the power band for the next gear up. Do it too soon and you will only have to change down again. When changing up, try to do so quickly. Having a few revs to spare will take care of the speed drop as you release the accelerator to change gears.

It may all sound obvious, but so many people make the mistake of 'trying to see if the car will go any faster'. If you misjudge it, the speed losses for every abortive change will combine and the engine revs will fall too far below maximum torque for the engine to have anywhere near full power. If this happens, the only power you will find will be in a low gear, and depending on the ratios of your gear box, that is where you will stay.

BRAKING

If you can reduce your speed without losing control of your car, you are a long way toward minimising damage to both the car and its occupants, and the easiest way to do this is simply to take your foot off the accelerator pedal. Wind resistance against a vehicle/caravan combination is considerable, and, as long as there is no engine driving them, this resistance, combined with any other form of drag, will slow down the car and caravan in a surprisingly short distance. It's not nearly as simple as it sounds, though. Having slowed down enough, what the driver must do is try to control the car for a few seconds until the speed is low enough for controlled braking and a complete stop.

OVERTAKING

Overtaking other vehicles also requires great care, as well as a greatly enhanced sphere of awareness. There is no substitute for knowing your vehicle. Doing the arithmetic can sometimes bring it all home to you. A vehicle travelling at 100kph covers just under 28m in a second. If it takes you 20 seconds to pass another vehicle you will have covered 554m in that time – just over half a kilometre. If another vehicle is coming towards you, the two vehicles travelling at their relatively safe speeds approach each other at a combined 200kph! Someone with knowledge of ballistics could work out the velocities, and they are sure to be terrifying.

Make sure you have a good view ahead and that no one is doing stupid things behind you. Only make your move when the vehicle you are about to overtake is aware of your intentions and not planning to accelerate at the same time.

(No matter how good his intentions, if a truck driver with an elevated view of the road waves you on, he may not be judging the situation correctly. Consider this seriously before hitting the accelerator.)

CHAPTER SIX

MOTORHOMES

The luxury motorhome must surely represent the ultimate touring vehicle. As a combination of large vehicle and caravan it offers the benefits of both, and allows the traveller the sort of freedoms one would usually find only on a yacht! Passengers, for example, are able to sleep comfortably stretched out while the kilometres speed by.

Modern motorhomes are made for comfort, lightness and aerodynamic efficiency – they're certainly more evolved than their older relatives. The interior layouts are more sophisticated and well thought out and the specification levels are higher. Although a common complaint is that the smaller versions are underpowered, fuel consumption is an important aspect of touring; while bigger engines have more power and are more exciting to drive, they are very much thirstier.

DIESEL TECHNOLOGY

High speed and rapid acceleration are not important in a motorhome, so it will come as no surprise to learn that diesel engines are commonly fitted to the larger models. New technology has seen these engines become smoother and quieter, and they've always been more fuel-efficient and longer lasting than petrol engines. They also require less servicing, so are far cheaper to run. Diesel-powered vehicles are more robustly made to handle the higher compression ratios – and an added bonus is that diesel is lead-free.

CAMPER UNITS

If you already own a bakkie, the cheapest, quickest and certainly easiest option is to buy a pick-up camper unit. These contain a bunk bed and small kitchenette and simply bolt onto the load area in place of the canopy. The unit stands on strong retractable legs, which support its full weight on the ground so that the vehicle can be reversed underneath to make loading easier. Once at your destination the legs provide stability, and you can simply drive out from under it instead of hauling it around with you. It does not rely on the support of the parent vehicle and can be lived in as is.

CAMPER 'VANS'

Among the smaller vehicles that can be called motorhomes are the Kombis or Microbuses that have been converted into 'campers'. Their seating is replaced with custom-made interiors, and their designers make maximum use of every inch of the interior space, with fold-up double bunks, small bar-type fridges and gas cookers. Washing up is done in a plastic basin. Colourful curtains seem to be obligatory, providing privacy and relief from the sun – and generally making for a happier-looking vehicle.

For the couple who needs only the bare essentials and does not wish to spend much money, there are still second-hand ones to be found in good condition. But do be cautious of temptingly low prices: campers are slightly heavier than the normal vehicle, so greater strain is put on CV joints, clutches and suspension. Repair and replacement is an expensive exercise. Have these areas checked thoroughly by a reputable dealer, and if there is significant wear, negotiate a better price.

Special roofs give camper conversions much-needed headroom. One style resembles the 'pop-top' caravan, while another hinges on one side, lifting up to reveal a wedge-shaped tent with windows that gives more headroom, although the highest point is to one side. A big advantage of the Kombi-style motor home is that the modifications affect only the interior; apart from the slightly raised roof section, the outside is no bigger than that of the normal vehicle. This makes for easy parking and driving around town.

MEDIUM-SIZED MOTORHOMES

Many of the medium-sized motorhomes owe their ancestry to delivery vehicles or trucks, as the powerful chassis and capacious load areas are ideal platforms for the caravan-like interiors. The power-to-weight ratios are well suited to this type of vehicle, and features such as double-back wheels, originally designed for industrial use, give added stability and extra traction on the highway. The cabs are cleverly compact while retaining all the creature comforts for a driver who spends many hours a day on the road.

All large motorhomes come with power steering, although the more horizontal angle of the steering wheel takes some getting used to. Reversing is a lot easier than with a caravan, but some motorhomes have 'feelers' fitted to the rear corners to assist the driver when parking in a restricted space. The suspension is something like that of a luxury bus, and many have automatic gearboxes. Tyres are designed for a softer ride than that of the ancestral truck or delivery vehicle, and brakes are power-assisted.

INTERIOR LAYOUTS

Allowances always have to be made for the cab, of course, but there are nevertheless many interior options. In some interiors, the driver and co-driver's seats are able to swivel around to face two or more back seats, forming a small lounge. (The seats lock into place, so they cannot swivel while you're zooming along a highway. Be sure to check that the mechanisms are holding firmly before setting off!)

Where the bodywork extends the length of the vehicle, the space directly above the cab is often used for sleeping. In certain motorhome models a double bunk is lowered to just above the steering wheel, to give the occupants easier access. Otherwise the interior simply extends above the cab and access is provided via steps. When not used for sleeping this becomes a very handy storage area, as it is removed from the main thoroughfare.

The living area of the motorhome tends to be built around the front end of the vehicle – the engine needs to be accessible from various angles for servicing, and one of these may be from inside the cab. Access to the cab is made easier by the fact that there is already a side entrance, and in these cases access to the driver's seat will be via the living area. Some cabs do not depart much from their industrial origins and access here is gained via an ordinary door on each side. Depending on the country of origin, many imported motorhomes have the steering wheel and door on the 'wrong' side for South African roads. While this is not illegal, it does mean that the driver will have to make allowances for restricted vision. If you don't like the idea, rather buy a locally made vehicle.

A welcome feature common to medium to large motorhomes is the elevated vantage point from inside the vehicle. In the larger motorhomes this is quite pronounced, as the wheels are of a greater diameter and the engine higher. This provides a much-improved view of the scenery and of the road ahead. The largest vehicles have tall, bus-like windows that provide expansive views, and the high-backed seats with armrests make driving a pleasure.

INCREASING YOUR MOBILITY

One of the limitations of a motorhome is the lack of mobility once camp has been set up. If you leave in your motorhome it can mean losing your site, so many owners bring along extra transport.

Bicycles are very popular as they are light, easy to dismantle and ideal for making short trips into town or the surrounding countryside. With modern cycle gearing it is possible to travel far with comparatively little effort, and it is enjoyable to see the countryside from close up (while getting gentle exercise for free!). With the correct security measures you can park a bicycle almost anywhere, and it is not unusual to see them travelling in lifts!

The more adventurous (or lazy) may opt for a motorbike (or two). You may need to have a special compartment or trailer, and in any event most motorbikes will probably be too wide for a passageway. If you do manage to park your bike inside, there is still the possibility of oil leaking onto your carpets. Because of the weight of even a medium-sized bike, you will need an adequate loading ramp and at least two strong pairs of hands to hold and guide it during loading.

If you are fortunate enough to own a large motorhome as well as a small, light car, the easiest thing to do is to tow the car along behind you. All you need is the right towing apparatus and you'll have all the transport you want at your destination. If this sounds extravagant, consider that one of the largest makes in Europe, the Volvo-based Vario Perfect 1200, even provides inside parking for a Ferrari 355 Spyder! The price in the UK was £444,000 (without the Ferrari) in 1998. Weight? A mere 18 tons.

The luxury motorhomes by WJ. represent the top of the range in South Africa and are superb in almost every respect. As true custom-built vehicles they are designed for luxury travel of the highest standard and the list of specifications and features is long. Although their dimensions put them in the largest class of recreational vehicle, they are seldom designed to accommodate more than two couples. Handling is effortless and the atmosphere inside is one of restrained elegance.

CARING FOR YOUR SECOND HOME

When your motorhome is not in use, remember that it still needs care. Engines, tyres and batteries were not designed to be left standing for any length of time, and if they do, accelerated deterioration takes place. Tyres may develop flat spots, the battery will corrode internally and light rust may form on areas devoid of oil. This will not happen in just a few weeks, but after six months you'll notice the differences.

The best option is to take your motorhome for a short drive once or twice a month, just far enough to get all fluids and lubricants circulating well and to give the battery a light charge. If this is not possible, the vehicle should be jacked up and put on blocks.

Batteries are designed to be used, and unless they are charged and discharged on a regular basis, there is no flow in the acid, the plates inside start to buckle and the battery will begin to deteriorate. If your motorhome or caravan is left standing for any length of time, you should discharge the battery by connecting the two terminals to a light bulb and letting it burn for several hours. The battery will now be in a state of discharge and will register a low reading if connected to a voltmeter. Once a month, recharge it for five hours with a trickle charger from your nearest accessory shop.

A good tip is to buy the same size battery as the one you have in your car and swap the two around once a month. This will prolong the life of both batteries, and will also ensure you have a spare in the case of one battery failing.

The engine should be left to run for 10 minutes every two or three weeks and the gearbox put through all the gears. Brake fluid should be changed regularly once a year

Few people get to spend more than a few weeks a year on vacation, and even going away every weekend can get tiresome. Considering the cost of a motorhome and the amount of time it will actually be used, it makes good sense to share the cost and use of it with one or more interested parties. Many people do this with holiday homes, caravans and boats. It takes a responsible and mature attitude for this to work, and an honest and caring partnership should be a minimum requirement, but if it makes for more holidays and weekends for more people at a greatly reduced cost, then it is surely well worth a try.

CHAPTER SEVEN

LIGHTING

Never before has the outdoor enthusiast had such a wide range of lighting to choose from. There's a system to suit any pocket and lifestyle, but it is not only a case of which system – it's more often a matter of how many. A good torch will provide you with light (and cost a fortune in batteries), but if one of the party has to visit the ablution block late at night, for example, the unfortunate others will be left in the total darkness only the African bush can provide. Tent campers therefore need to have two kinds of lights: a reliable torch for finding things and a lamp that provides good, even light cheaply for hours at a time.

CANDLES

The humble, low-cost wax candle still holds the highest and lowest positions on the scale of desirable lighting. The romance of a candlelit dinner table has no equal, yet during a power failure, the candle is merely a messy, flickering back-up.

But candles have other, in-between uses. They're so simple as to be totally foolproof. You can break them up into pieces to make several smaller candles, or use the wax as lubrication or waterproofing (when warmed in water, wax is as malleable and sticky as clay and can seal off leaky patches in tents or caravans). And if you are caught far from a tackle shop, a ball of wax can even be used as a fishing float. Molten wax can also fuel a fire (and stain your clothes!).

The downside of candles is that for the tent dweller they are dangerous, as the naked flame is a threat to inflammable fabrics. Without protective glass, outdoor candles can be impossible in even a light breeze;

they produce erratic light – and one that's a great aid to eyestrain!

Burn rate is the thing to look for in candles. Some are more 'fatty' than others (to the trained eye they appear whiter and 'waxier'), and while these produce spectacular drip patterns, they do not last as long as the more clean-burning variety.

A variety of small candle-holders are made for outdoor use. Some are beautifully made tall brass lanterns – hardy and reassuringly resilient – that offer low-intensity light for camping or boating. Remember that brightness is not always a sought-after attribute, as it can be rather blinding. The pressed-tin holders are cheap, light and do their job well.

HURRICANE LAMPS

Paraffin hurricane lamps are still popular, and offer one of the hardiest forms of lighting around. They're also comparatively cheap to buy and run, and come in a variety of sizes and colours.

The main drawback, however, is that they get very hot on top. Pick them up by the wire handle only, which must be left folded down when the lamp is standing on a table. They don't get as hot if they're left hanging from a wire hook, though – probably because the heat is carried away more efficiently. And, of course, there is not much danger of them being knocked over.

Hurricane lamps certainly live up to their name – test them out if you're ever plagued by wind on a dark night and need to visit the loo!

When used turned right down as a night light, they will burn till morning on a surprisingly small amount of paraffin. You may wish to keep a small one expressly for this purpose.

Hurricane lamps have a weak point at the seams where the upper framework is fixed to the storage tank. If they get banged about these joints tend to work loose and leak – the telltale sign is a slowly growing pool of paraffin around the base. This is easily repaired with a thin flame and a bit of solder, but can be a nuisance till you get it seen to.

PRESSURE LAMPS

Pressure lamps also run on paraffin, and are light, strong and portable – the Coleman version is the lamp by which all other lamps are judged!

These lamps use the same mantle system as ordinary gas lamps do: atomised paraffin heated in a small tank and pumped in under pressure to provide the fuel. The effect of the combined heat and pressure in the tank changes the liquid paraffin into gas by the time it reaches the mantle. This provides a light that is as bright as that of any gas lamp but a lot more portable, as it has a much smaller reservoir of fuel. This is no limitation, though, as a full tank of paraffin (about a litre) will burn brightly for up to eight hours. It burns with a gentle hiss, and over the years the green enamel and silver finish of the Coleman has become synonymous with reliability and endurance. Coleman lamps are expensive, but you will be enjoying them long after you have forgotten what they cost.

There is a large, chrome-plated version of a Coleman made in the Far East. It has a pressure gauge on the reservoir and a large metal lampshade that rests on the area surrounding the upper tank, giving it a more rustic look. These lamps provide the same amount of light as the smaller pressure-lamp models, but for some reason do not enjoy the same reputation as the Coleman. Coleman is widely distributed, so the preference may have something to do with the availability of spare parts. If you are going off-road, carry two spare glasses.

GAS

When you're living outdoors, you're likely to find that Low Pressure Gas (LPG) is your primary fuel; it's probably the only viable alternative to electricity. It is cheap, clean (it burns with no residue or smell), easily obtainable and provides a powerful light.

Gas is sold by weight and stored in metal gas cylinders or 'bottles', as they are commonly known (their size is denoted by the weight of gas they contain). The most popular sizes are the 3,7kg and 10kg bottles as well as the ultra-light cartridges used by hikers. Caravans and motorhomes often use 20kg cylinders, and although these are fairly heavy they do contain enough gas to last a long time

The range of gas lights is fairly elementary, and by clever use of standard fittings the same lamp head can be connected to all bottles and a variety of extension tubes, which can be fitted to a braai skottel or grill. There are a number of makes, all of them reliable.

The lamp head itself consists of a thin metal frame and lid holding a glass cylinder to protect the fragile mantle. The gas is fed in from below through a pipe and into the mantle, which works in the same way as the Coleman. It provides a bright yet restful light, burning with the characteristic hiss of a pressure lamp. The gas from the cylinder is released by turning a valve. When you are connecting the fittings, check that the lamp is not leaking: paint on a thin layer of soapy water; if there are leaks, you will see the bubbles forming. Always carry a spare valve 'key', spare washers and a couple of spare mantles.

A word about mantles. When they're new, they are small silky bags in various shapes (some have one hole, some have two) that attach to the feed pipe for the fuel. They are tied on by a thin cord around a collar. Before they will operate, they need to be incinerated in situ: light them with a match or lighter and gently blow out the flame; a thin red line will creep over the surface and when the mantle is completely burned it will be quite white. Do not touch it from now on or it will disintegrate. When you light the lamp, the mantle will 'pop' and burn brightly. Small tears are nothing to worry about, but when these enlarge, fit a new one.

ELECTRICITY

If you have access to electricity it may seem silly to use any other power source. Ordinary garden lights are becoming very popular, as they're lightweight and purpose-made for outdoor use. And they don't get hot or hiss.

If they are of the low-voltage variety they are as safe as you can reasonably expect to get. They are not designed to be carried about much, but provide so much lighting that this hardly seems necessary – they usually have several bulbs on a single cord.

TORCHES

Torches with rechargeable batteries are a great innovation. Some can be left permanently on charge, only being taken off the charging bracket to be used. They do require a permanent power source though. Others have a combination of lights: a neon light to produce an even, all-over light with faint shadows for reading; a bulb and reflector to produce a beam; and a red or orange flashing light for breakdowns or emergencies. The Baygen wind-up torch is a most wonderful thing as it works off a small dynamo and therefore requires no batteries at all.

Standing torches are a very good idea as they free your hands for other tasks. Some have large magnets, so can be stuck onto a metal surface (Prestik is a handy aid, too).

Traditional cylindrical torches are still the most popular make – the Maglite is the industry standard. These torches come in a wide range of sizes, from a tiny single-cell version that is literally key-ring size to the large, many-celled, heavy-duty versions. With bodies made from aircraft-grade aluminium and sealed with strong O-rings in high viscosity grease, they are quite water- and dust-proof, and have variable beams that can be focused. They use special bulbs that can take severe punishment (a spare is stored in the handle). No serious 'outdoor-type' should be without one.

LIGHT STICKS

On the 'outer edges' of lighting methods we find light-sticks, which are very useful in emergencies. They work on chemicals that fluoresce strongly when mixed to produce a strong green glow. Very small versions exist that are used to attract fish to bait at night, but the larger variety is capable of dimly lighting up a small room.

As a rule, they are not much good for anything other than signalling or marking your position – the slightly unearthly light is instantly recognisable, even at a distance.

CHAPTER EIGHT

THE OUTDOOR KITCHEN

There is something about a meal prepared over an open fire that has a special quality, and it is not surprising that there is a huge industry that caters to this pastime. After wood, Low Pressure Gas (LPG) is the most popular source of energy for cooking outdoors, and a wide range of accessories has evolved to cater for this market, too.

If you are a keen outdoor cook and see preparing food as a creative outlet, you could easily get carried away at a well-stocked accessories store. But do beware, for enthusiastic proponents of any activity are grist to the marketing mill, and you could end up with a lot of fancy looking stuff that does very little except empty your wallet. Fortunately there are just as many worthwhile products, from humble cutting boards and ultra-light, go-anywhere hiker's stoves to the most sophisticated generator-driven deep freezes, all of which help to make the outdoor kitchen a satisfying place in which to be.

FIXED STOVES

Most camping and caravan stoves are powered by gas, which is relatively cheap and easily obtainable at garages, hardware stores and general dealers. Gas instantly produces a flame, so no energy is wasted waiting for the element to heat up.

Permanent stoves such as those in caravans have two, three or four burners, and each burner has its own on/off 'switch' (this is usually a safety valve and regulator in one). The dial is friction-fitted onto a spring-loaded shaft, and when pushed in and turned will allow a variable flow of gas to reach a burner. When returned to the 'off' position the regulator will spring back and shut off the flow of gas. Any small spark will ignite the flame, so watch those fingers when lighting up!

PORTABLE GAS STOVES

The simplest device to fit onto a gas cylinder is a 'cooker top'. It is cheap, can easily support a large pot and fits directly onto the gas cylinder. Pressure is regulated by opening or closing the valve on the cylinder.

An attachment that holds a normal lamp head can be fitted under the cooker top, which gives you heat for cooking and a good strong light to see by. Skottel pans and cast-iron grills are other popular gas cylinder attachments. Extension tubes lift the work surfaces to a more convenient height and metal feet provide a more substantial base to hold it upright.

If you are a keen hiker or simply don't like to carry cumbersome things, the small, fold-up gas burners that run off gas 'cartridges' could be just the thing for you. A convenient cartridge is inserted under the burner and provides a stand as well as a small reservoir of gas. Canisters range in size from 190–450g.

On some cooker tops, a hard spike protrudes inside a rubber seal, which will puncture the canister as you clip it in place; other canisters screw onto the fitting. You will need to carry a supply of canisters with you, but these weigh very little and one will provide all the heat you need to prepare a hearty meal.

Hikers will appreciate the convenience and efficiency of gas, particularly in wet or windy conditions.

PRESSURE STOVES

The small, liquid-fuelled pressure stoves run on paraffin, petrol, benzine or methylated spirits, and some of the more advanced multi-fuel models have a choice of jets that allow them to run on all three: petrol, benzine or paraffin. Each cooker consists of a small fuel tank that is filled with compressed air via a small hand pump. The compressed air pushes the liquid fuel into the reservoir system that surrounds the outlet in such a way that any flame it produces pre-heats the liquid on its way to the jet. The

> ## TAKING A LEAK
> Gas leaks in confined spaces are dangerous. If you are not going to use your gas appliance for any length of time, turn off the gas supply at the cylinder as an extra precaution. Gas detectors do work, but are no substitute for a careful owner. If your stove does not allow for the flame to be turned down very low, rest assured – this is a safety feature. A very low flame can easily be blown out, and if this had to happen while the stove was unattended, your caravan could quickly fill with gas. The explosion as you try to relight the stove would be heard kilometres away.

heated fuel is 'atomised' as it exits the tiny opening, producing a fine, hot vapour that burns readily. Fuels become highly flammable in this state and the stove will burn happily until the supply runs out. The amount of heat produced by each type of fuel varies, but all of them are roughly in the same temperature band, which makes them ideal for cooking.

No pressure stoves are totally safe and, like any fire, should never be left burning unattended. Because the flame is under pressure, it is much harder to put out; this is a valuable safety feature when it's windy, but if the flame does go out for any reason, fuel may squirt out and saturate anything nearby. This is extremely dangerous, and is one reason why you should never cook in a tent. If the flame does go out, release the pressure as quickly as you can. Even when it's not under pressure, hot fuel is more prone to ignition than cold. Conflagration can be induced by the very smallest of sparks and the results can be devastating. The safety aspect cannot be over-emphasised – remember that you're also likely to be very far from help.

When choosing a hiking stove, look at the design of the burner itself. One type looks something like a small inverted showerhead, with three or four surrounding arms to support lightweight pots or pans; others resemble the head of a Primus stove. In all of them the idea is to distribute the gas to produce a broad ring of flame that spreads out to heat the underside of the pot. The Primus type of system relies on a relatively high pressure to keep burning efficiently. The amount of heat can be controlled to a certain extent by releasing pressure via a small valve.

More evolved versions have sophisticated wind-deflectors that surround the central gas outlet, so even in a strong wind the flame cannot be blown out from under the pot. Cookers built this way work extremely well. Although they are certainly not cheap, their true worth cannot be measured in rands and cents. Some have a detachable fuel bottle, which can be carried upright and safely sealed in backpacks. Well-known and reliable makes are Primus, Petromax, MSR, Optimus and Coleman.

It must be said that fashion plays a significant role in many things, and it's not always practicality or value for money that is the deciding factor – the ordinary Primus pressure stoves used in rural households in South Africa are a good example. They're about twice the size of their smaller cousins, are every bit as efficient and run for much longer. Spare parts are cheap and widely available and they cost a fraction of the price of the purpose-made camping or hiking stove. The only drawback is that they're slightly heavier. Such stoves were popular among the boating fraternity in the early 1900s, and they remain attractive in their shiny brass livery. They even offer a choice of heads – the 'silent' head emits nothing more than a gentle hiss when burning. If you are camping on a limited budget or do not want to spend more than you need to on expensive equipment that may get damaged on a particularly rough trip, they will prove their worth. (Speaking of fashion, exactly the opposite has happened with the black cast-iron 'potjie', which your grandmother would not have been seen dead cooking in.)

NO-PRESSURE STOVES

The pressed-tin paraffin stoves made by Panda or Diamond burn a large round or double wick, and you can adjust the heat from very hot to warm. They cost much less than a conventional Primus and come in a range of perfectly acceptable colours.

Some people may find the slightly oily smell of the paraffin stove unpleasant at first, but this fuel remains popular because it is not highly inflammable (unless it is absorbed into a wick of some sort, it will not burn at all – a match thrown into a bucket of it will have no effect other than to put out the match). It is also more easily available than gas or petrol. Travellers to rural areas can rely on finding paraffin anywhere. It is also a good metal-cleaning agent in the event of a breakdown and can, in desperate situations, be used as an insect repellent. It tastes appalling and will repel all but the keenest humans as well, so take care.

The simpler alcohol stoves are not as popular as they should be. They are very light and require no pressure, so they get a diminished 'danger rating'. They are also easy to light, burn quite silently and produce a distinct but fortunately faint odour. The deep-blue flame produces a sharp clean heat, and if you run out of the usual fuel, they will run – although not quite as well – on a good double tot of whisky or brandy! Alcohol evaporates quickly and it is these escaping vapours that burn. The longer it burns, the hotter the metal of the stove gets and the more vapour the liquid gives off. You will notice the flame slowly getting bigger as the process continues. To put the flame out, simply pop the lid on. As it's sensitive to a good supply of air, it will go out immediately.

Lower down the scale in terms of sophistication are the very small solid-fuel stoves, which run on small, domino-shaped tablets of combustible material. A typical example, such as the one made by Esbit, will support a light pot when snapped open into cooking mode, and when folded into its box shape is about the size of a paperback novel. These stoves produce limited heat, and the volume of which is controlled by the number of fuel tablets (they work best for smallish quantities of food or water). If you are planning on cooking a meal on one, make sure you have a good supply of tablets handy. The fuel is clean-burning and produces no smoke and very little odour, but it is comparatively expensive.

Most models are made from light-gauge metal, and as a result they do not stay hot for long – a real boon when packing up to go.

The simplest, cheapest and easiest fuel for heating has to be spirit jelly. Sold in a container something like a syrup tin, the jelly is the same translucent electric purple as methylated spirits, and is set alight with a match or lighter. It produces the same type of heat and flame as an alcohol stove does, and is put out in the same way. The tins come in a range of sizes from 250ml to five litres (the larger one is meant more for refilling the smaller tins than for carrying around). The tins have no fold-out legs or supports of any kind, so you will need something sturdy on which to stand your pot or pan.

FRIDGES AND FREEZERS

The portable fridge or freezer is fast becoming an essential rather than a luxury item. The heat of the African summer makes this perfectly understandable, and we can only wonder why it took this marvellous invention so long to penetrate the market the way it has. A freezer should, by definition, be able to freeze water, i.e. it must be able to reach 0°C – freezing point or below. A fridge will keep the contents cold, at least well below room temperature, but will not be able to freeze water to make ice.

Portable fridges and freezers are the only large appliances powered by 12 volt, 220 volt or gas, so they can be operated anywhere from the baking sands of the Kalahari to the cooler Western Cape.

Most useful to the tent-dweller and widely used by the 4x4 fraternity and safari industry, they can also be installed in holiday homes isolated from an electrical power supply. When not being used on vacation, they can do duty as a spare fridge at home – their size is perfect for vehicle, office, guest room or study use. Because they have no motors they are absolutely silent.

Some models may offer only the electrical option. But if you are a regular visitor to resorts that have electrical power points, it doesn't make sense to pay for an option that you may never use, such as gas.

When you're buying a fridge, find out about the thickness of the insulation. Along with the freezing power of the unit, this is what physically isolates the inside storage area from the temperature outside.

Most of the smaller models have walls roughly the same thickness as a large, efficient cooler box, and this is essentially what they are – powered cooler boxes, running off a 12-volt power supply. They will be perfectly efficient in temperatures of about 28°C or 30°C, but could start to be sorely tested as the temperature climbs into the mid-30s and over. Any higher than that and all they'll be able to do is keep the inside several degrees lower than the temperature outside. If the outside temperature reaches 45°C, don't be surprised to find the entire contents spoiled.

Some 'fridges' can be set to heat food, which is wonderful if you need to keep bottles warm for babies. Fridges with this feature are small by comparison with other makes and are easy to take on picnics.

If you are going to an area where the daily temperatures regularly exceed 35°C, consider buying a unit with thicker insulation. It will cost more, but extreme conditions require more capable machines. Most of the heavier-duty models are top-loaders with thick, insulated lids – this method of access stops more cold air from escaping. The coldest part will be right at the bottom, so pack your fridge with this in mind. Either keep the things you use most on top or use supplies from the top down.

Whether fridge or freezer, open it as little as possible. Generally speaking, metal containers will get colder more quickly than plastic ones, so bear this in mind when storing things. If you want to make ice in a top-loading freezer, you will have to unpack everything to get to the coldest part at the bottom, or be content to wait longer for it to freeze closer to the top. The latter is the best idea, especially if you have meat or fish stored at the bottom. Plan ahead and put in the tray in time.

EATING OUT

Many more people are learning to appreciate the wonders of an evening spent over a carefully prepared meal in a well-chosen setting.

Not content with having it done for them (for a fee) at some expensive restaurant, many outdoor enthusiasts create the experience for themselves. Its success has a lot to do with one's general attitude to life. It would be misleading to imply that every meal should take place at a candlelit table with crystal glasses and iced champagne. To the committed outdoors enthusiast, though, being in a spectacular natural setting beats any restaurant any day.

Setting an attractive table requires skill, but this does not mean spending hours arranging everything and making it a chore. The creation of atmosphere will come as a result of careful choices on your part. Setting it all out should never take more than a few minutes.

TABLES

The ideal table has enough space for a place setting for everyone, is sturdy enough to provide a stable platform and should be able to double up as a work surface while the meal is being prepared. It must be a good enough surface for reading and writing and should be light enough to be moved around easily, and it must fold up when it needs to be stored. Like most things, if it is well designed and does the job, it will automatically look good as well.

Decide whether you're going to get one main table – to be used for anything and everything – or a secondary table with a specialised use.

Smaller, slatted tables work well on picnics, as they offer standing room for bottles and bowls. The air spaces between the slats add to their lightness. They can be small and shaky, though, and are not great to eat at; even a small bump can upset the entire contents.

It can also be difficult to stand a wine glass or salt cellar upright on a surface where the gaps are as large as the supports. A plastic table cloth may disguise this, and while it is no solution to the problem, it will keep spilled liquids off legs and clothing.

Large plastic tables, designed originally as garden furniture for the home, have become very popular as their size, lightness and ease of assembly is almost unrivalled. They are cheaper than many smaller or heavier options, and as they're plastic can be kept sparkling clean with a wash every now and then. All things considered, they are good value for money and an excellent solution to having dinner outdoors.

Another useful style of table is one made of aluminium tubing and Formica. They fold up into something rather like a large, flat suitcase and can be carried around with a handle. For their size they are not cheap, but they are very light and easy to pack. Also in the fold-up department is the four-seater table-and-chair variety with a hole in the middle of the table for an umbrella. They are great for picnics but the hinges tend to be fragile, and once broken they are not easy to repair.

The more industrial-style tables have legs that fold up into their shallow, box-shaped, spot-welded tops. When fully open, the legs are braced with an elbow that effectively locks them in place. They are rather heavy and very strong; they can support the full weight of an adult. If this sounds like overkill, consider the large family (or two) that spends three weeks at a single venue with many small children. The stability and sheer weight of these tables provide a safe platform for gas cookers and boiling-hot pots. Despite their size, these tables fall into the 'single use' category and are best left in situ. They stand up to rigorous treatment and the peace of mind gained from knowing they cannot be accidentally knocked over by a small child more than outweighs their limitations in terms of lightness and portability.

Several fold-up TV tables are a versatile alternative to one large table, and won't take up as much permanent space.

CHAIRS

The most important thing to look for in a chair is lower-back support and one of the chairs that provides this best is the humble, canvas and metal-framed fishermen's chair. At first glance it may look like a chair made for a child, but the fold-down back panel is cleverly positioned to suit most human frames. They are much appreciated by fishermen who may have to spend many long hours in them waiting for dinner to bite.

A chair made from alloy tubing with a waterproof fabric cover is strong and easy to store. It can weigh very little more – and in some cases less – than its plastic poolside counterpart, although you would not say so to look at them. The metal frames are hardwearing and the fabric and through-fittings are easy and cheap to replace, which gives each chair a long working life.

Wooden chairs are probably the nicest looking, and are often made from good hardwoods. They tend to be found at the more upmarket shops and may even have inviting-looking sun shades and arm rests. Their associations lie with mailships and an altogether grander era of travel. For the modern traveller they have their drawbacks: depending on where the cross-pieces fall, you may have to move about frequently to remain comfortable. Compared to other types of chairs they can be heavy, and if left out in the rain can warp and become difficult to fold. The poolside folding plastic deck chair is right up there with the plastic garden table in terms of lightness and convenience. Plastic also doesn't get as cold as metal, so is easier on the skin.

If you're considering fabric-upholstered outdoor chairs, bear in mind that when the fabric stretches, the position of the occupant is lowered, and all previous areas of support move up and become less effective.

White reflects light as well as heat, which is why the upper surfaces of most airliners are painted that colour. Any white accessory should therefore last longer and be easier to handle than any darker colour. Chalk up another point for garden furniture!

Another important aspect of any chair is its height in relation to the table. This will not be a problem with the garden-table owner, as the chairs are often sold as part of a set. Most deck chairs – made for reclining in – are a fraction too low to be used at most tables.

SETTING THE TABLE

Wicker holders with good-quality paper plates are attractive and perfectly adequate for most meals. The better-quality plates do not absorb moisture, and can be patterned, in plain colours or just plain white. They may appear flimsy at first, but once in their holders they are quite firm and can also be used for holding rolls, chips and fruit. And washing-up will be reduced to a quick walk to the bin! If you are using the thinner white variety and a certain meal ends up looking too juicy, simply use a double layer of plates.

Full dinner sets of Melamine (a strong, well-tried material) are readily available. The styling is usually attractively low-key but the subdued tones belie the resilience of the material. The strength-to-weight ratio is high and pieces can fall hard without suffering any damage. You will need to do the washing-up after every meal, but will also have the satisfaction of eating out of a better class of receptacle.

More quality stainless-steel plates are being made than ever before. The finishes and the designs are better, and stainless steel is, to all intents and purposes, everlasting. There is even a range of surprisingly thin and light plates and cups for hikers – a good choice for anyone.

Large wooden salad bowls may be attractive but they're generally made from heavy woods, so are best left at home. The new plastic versions are often larger and always more colourful, with a variety of finishes from gloss to satin to bold tropical print. They are not that expensive and can be bought in packs. Their walls are thin, so you can usually stack five or so in not much more space than you would one. Colour co-ordinated spoons can be bought, too.

In the plastic department you will find a wide range of wineglasses, mugs, tumblers and containers. To the connoisseur, wine loses something if drunk out of anything other than glass, but crystal is not a good survivor of long journeys.

Enamel mugs have been around for many years and with the advent of the new South Africa they have become a bit of a fashion statement. They are hardwearing, cheap by any standards and do not alter the taste of anything, including wine. Experienced campers swear by them as they can hold every type of liquid. As long as they are clean when you fill them, you should detect no contamination at all. The pale yellow, powder blue or green with black trim – or, even better, white with kitsch flower patterns – are the classic themes and they come in a variety of sizes. The modern ranges have sophisticated colour schemes and include tea cups or small coffee cups, both with matching saucers. A final touch, if you can find them, are the matching enamel spoons.

A good supply of brightly coloured paper party cups can be fun for children to use, and matching paper napkins add a nice touch. Dishes with lids will stop things getting into the butter or margarine, and salt and pepper cellars with snap-on lids and bottoms are a must if you are camping at the coast. Salt attracts moisture and unless you can keep it out, your salt will become unpourable within hours. Putting rice grains in the container will have little or no effect. As a rule, choose containers with vacuum-seal lids as they insulate the contents against humidity, heat or cold. Decant any supplies from glass bottles into strong, sealable containers before you leave.

Keeping wine cool will be no problem as long as you have a good supply of ice and an ice bucket. Clay coolers work well at home but are too heavy and fragile to be taken on holiday. A good plastic insulator that fits the bottle will work well if the wine is put in straight out of the fridge. If you run out of ice, wrap wine bottles in damp newspaper and stand the bottle in a draught. Keep the paper wet until the wine is ready to be opened.

The aroma of filter coffee in the bush is irresistible – fortunately, lightweight plastic filter holders are easy to use. They come in either two-cup or four-cup models. Take plenty of filters and a flask of hot water with you on the road and enjoy a good cup or two while you journey.

KITCHEN UTENSILS

There is nothing wrong with taking all your implements along with you, but with a little thought you can probably get away with less. The secret lies in the versatility of certain implements: a good chef can do many things with a small knife, from peeling a potato to coring an apple to dicing carrots. Many of us are either too rushed to acquire these skills or, more likely, do not see the need to do so if there is a purpose-made implement for the task.

KNIVES

A small knife with a blade of between 5–10cm is a must in any kitchen. A shorter blade is easier around corners and will do most of the lighter tasks. It can also be used for peeling, if you are up to it, although a short blade (5cm) is best for this. A medium-length (10–15cm blade) will be good for all the in-between tasks such as chopping carrots or slicing potatoes and onions. The longer the cut, the longer the blade, and for carving steaks and slicing chicken you will need a 20–25cm blade with a non-serrated edge. If you want to chop with that same knife you'll need a curved edge on a deeper blade – one that you can safely move up and down using the outside of your bent index finger as a guide, or in a rocking motion when dicing garlic or herbs. In professional parlance it's called a chef's knife and is a must-have for any even half-serious cook. Plan to have all three and there won't be much in the way of cutting that you won't be able to deal with.

Thicker, rigid blades are generally safer than thin, flexible ones. They are easier to control because they cut in predictable straight lines. The better makes have composite (usually black) or wood handles. If the metal of the blade extends the length of the knife it is called a 'full-tang' knife, and is the strongest configuration for a hand-held blade. (The 'tang' is the metal part behind the blade.) This makes for a robust design that, apart from lasting longer, should also feel good in your hand.

SHARPENING IMPLEMENTS

Thick-bladed knives are heavier and generally more expensive, and they need to be sharpened regularly. For this you will need a carborundum stone (or similar device), which is coarse on one side and smooth on the other. You'll also need to know how to use it. Although sharpening a knife on a stone is quite simple, it does take practice before you can do it really well. The reward for success is a razor-sharp blade that will be a pleasure to use.

For those brave enough to try, there are two types of stone – those lubricated with oil (which are harder and better suited for industrial use) and those lubricated with water. While both do the job well, the latter are cleaner in the kitchen. The stone itself is generally softer and bits will wear off during sharpening – just rinse the blade before

THE WOOD VS PLASTIC DEBATE

Have you ever wondered why you prefer a plastic cutting board but still use a wooden spoon?

There are many who believe that because wood is organic and its surface contains microscopic cracks and crevices, it is a perfect breeding ground for germs and other harmful bacteria. Most butchers, however, would disagree and some years ago a group of American scientists put this to the test.

Two cutting boards, one wood and one plastic, were placed in a laboratory at room temperature. A measured amount of bacteria was placed on the surface of each one and left for 24 hours. When examined under a microscope the following day, it was found that the bacteria on the wooden cutting board had all but died, while the bacteria on the plastic one had greatly multiplied.

According to the scientists, the reason was simple. Trees have been around for many millions of years, very much longer than most other organisms, and have evolved potent antibodies (chemicals) that are resistant to bacteria, the chief cause of decay. This is why wood does not decompose as quickly as most other organic substances, and that is why we use it for ships and homes, and furniture and cutting boards.

Not all woods have the same properties, though, and hardwoods are most resistant to bacteria. Cutting boards made from beech, saligna or other hardwoods can survive several human lifetimes of use. A wooden surface is also kinder on knife blades – and, of course, to many users it simply looks and feels better, too. For camping or caravanning, a nice thin one will do the job without weighing you down.

Please note: this is a controversial subject and opinions abound. Both wood and plastic types are freely available, so make up your own mind which cutting board you would rather use. In the meantime, though, don't throw away that wooden spoon!

using the knife. Both types of stone are available at good hardware stores. Another form of 'stone' is the efficient and lightweight diamond-impregnated metal plate, but you might have to search a bit to find one. Try the more specialised hardware stores.

Sharpening steels are used mainly by butchers, although you may find you have one with your carving set. These cylindrical grooved rods are made from very hard steel, hence the name, and when 'wiped' over a blade remove enough metal to sharpen it. In experienced hands they are quick to use and produce a very good edge. They also require no lubrication at all as they sharpen the blade 'dry'.

There are a great many patent devices on the market that will do the job of sharpening your cutlery. Some are just as efficient as the more traditional methods, but much depends on how easy you find them to use. None of the good ones are very cheap, though.

If you do not see yourself sharpening knives on a stone (this task seems always to get handed over to the men, somehow), consider this a major drawback and rather buy a knife with a thin, serrated self-sharpening blade.

In terms of ease of use, this type of knife is hard to beat, and somehow seems able to keep a sharp edge almost indefinitely. It will not be quite as robust as a thick-bladed knife, but a good make such as Washington Forge comes with a lifetime guarantee and, according to the makers, will also never need to be sharpened. The edge of the blade is designed in such a way that it sharpens itself as it wears down. It will never have quite the same edge as a well-honed carving knife, but it will be sharp enough for almost any task. Handles are generally hardwood and a light coat of cooking oil from time to time helps keep them in good shape and looking attractive.

OTHER 'MUST-HAVE' DEVICES

As useful as knives are, there are many other devices that are just as indispensable in the outdoor kitchen – and a good corkscrew, one that can get out the tightest cork, is one of them. It should be well made and have some sort of lever-action to provide maximum 'pull'. A good-quality egg-lifter is another – plastic for use with non-stick surfaces, but metal if you are planning on using it on toasted sandwiches over the fire as well. An egg-whisk is much lighter than an egg-beater and gives the beaten egg a foamier, lighter texture. Large dishing-up spoons (wood or metal) should have long handles and be deep enough to scoop up liquids. Salad spoons and forks can be flat and plastic, as they only come into contact with non-heated dishes. Always have a good bottle-opener handy – even though most bottles these days have screw-on tops. Have several dishcloths and allocate them specific jobs. Keep one that you don't mind getting dirty to lift the lid on the potjie, another to carry hot pots from stove to table, a third for hubby to wipe his hands on, and one to dry dishes with. This way you will always have at least one clean one! Different colours will stop the tribe from mixing them up.

A good-quality can opener will often come with other attachments built in. A bottle opener, a corkscrew and a lid lifter all-in-one means you won't spend as much time looking for these items. And a reliable vegetable peeler may double up as your short-blade knife, but I would not bet on the knife being quicker. Especially if you have a family, let the peeler do its job safely.

A good grater can be handy but is not essential – most things that end up getting grated work just as well sliced. Altering your cooking habits so that certain tasks become less time consuming is something you owe yourself on holiday.

You may decide to make up a longer (or shorter) list of your own. A mixer/mincer/shredder/liquidiser is not a utensil, although it does the job of several. It does not weigh a great deal, and if you have the space it is a wonderful time saver. Whatever it is, if it really makes a difference to your day, take it along.

OUTDOOR COOKING IMPLEMENTS

THE COOKING GRID

If there is one single outdoor accessory that stands head and shoulders above the rest in terms of simplicity and popularity, it is the humble braai grid. It appears in many forms, shapes, sizes and, more recently, materials. In its simplest form, as a flat piece of expanded metal sheeting (to give one version its proper name), it is not expensive at all and will give years – if not decades – of service. You can buy it in any length, width or thickness – the size and frequency of the openings are the final variable.

In its rough state, the sheeting will have many sharp corners and edges, so most outdoor cooks go for a slightly modified version with mild steel rod welded around the edge. The sharp edges are hammered over it to stop them from snagging bits of clothing. This also keeps the outside edge of the grid straight every time you clean it: do this by leaving it at the mercy of the flames for a few minutes just before they die out. The middle may buckle and bend slightly but once it has cooled down and you have given it a good 'going over' with a wire brush, simply hammer it flat again with a half-brick or flat stone. Avoid standing on it as you will walk the most impossible stains into your abode. Do not clean off the fat immediately after a braai, as this stops the grid from rusting; also don't rub the grid with newspaper, as the chemicals in the ink are not meant for human consumption.

Fold-up grids are a popular style, as you can turn everything on the fire at the same time. And as long as everything needs exactly the same treatment, that's fine, but if you habitually cook white and red meat together, you will know that a folding grid is not be the best option. The more discerning among us allow each piece of meat its own cooking time, and half the pleasure comes from carefully inspecting and assessing it before turning it over – or not.

Folding grids do have other advantages, though. They safeguard the dinner, as the contents are held firmly from above and below and cannot fall out of the sides. And as the metal wires that make up a folding grid are much thinner than the expanded metal-sheeting version, more of the meat is exposed to direct heat.

The latest grids are made from stainless steel. This wonderful material is very strong and looks good;

it's also practically everlasting and easy to clean. The best ones are electro-polished, which means that the finish is smoother than an abrasive-polished version. They are a lot more expensive, but unless it gets stolen you will probably never have to buy another one.

Grids come in many shapes and you will not have to look far to find one made to accommodate a large, medium or small fish, not to mention clever devices for baking potatoes and small grids for hikers that hold just enough meat for two.

You will also find them in a variety of finishes. The most common has a yellow, metallic finish that has been electro-plated with a non-corrosive coating. A black satin finish on a fish-shaped grid will probably be a non-stick coating, as fish skin tends to adhere strongly to bare metal when cooked over a fire.

It is important to have some sort of cover for your grid, especially since you will be travelling and packing it in and among other things. If there is nothing else available, use newspaper, which will isolate the greasiness, provided you use several layers. Green or black refuse bags are not up to the task as even the movement of the car can end up shredding them – with disastrously dirty results to whatever luggage was in contact with them. A heavy-duty PVC or plastic-impregnated canvas cover with strong press-studs on either side of the handle is the answer. Braai stains are particularly difficult to get out and the covers are not expensive.

THE CAST-IRON POTJIE

The cast-iron potjie is still with us, and although you can buy these pots 'in the raw', the ones treated with a vitreous enamel coating are the most healthy to eat from. You will not ingest any of the iron and they are much easier to clean.

They come in a wide variety of sizes; the smaller ones are referred to by volume and the larger ones are numbered. The smallest is the size of a small coffee cup and the largest could comfortably hold a large child. Numbers two and three are the most popular and hold enough food for a family of four or five.

Potjies are extremely versatile and can be used to make a wide variety of foods: porridge, scrambled eggs,

ANYONE FOR A SNACK?

The snack maker is a relatively cheap item that works really well over a fire. This wonderful invention consists of two circular moulds, hinged on one side and with two long handles that hold them closed on the other. You can make delicious toasted sandwiches in them and the number of fillings is limited only by your imagination. Make sure the moulds are well greased and each snack will fall out effortlessly.

soups, bread, spaghetti, stews and puddings. They can also be used to heat up liquids such as milk, although they are not built for easy pouring. If you plan to take only one pot with you, take a potjie, but make sure you clean it thoroughly between meals.

The enamel finish is susceptible to chipping, so always store it in its cardboard box and use only a wooden spoon to stir the contents.

The lid gets very hot, and although you can buy a variety of purpose-made implements to lift it, a damp cloth will work just as well.

The traditional device for keeping your potjie above the flames is a sturdy tripod with a chain hanging from the top. This allows you to start cooking before the fire has turned to coals. A large double-ended hook with one end through the handle and the other inserted into any link of the chain holds the pot at just the right height. The chain should be long enough for a wide range of heights; fine-tuning can be done by moving the feet of the tripod in or out. The legs of the tripod should not be at too steep an angle or your dinner may end up in the sand.

The three-legged potjie has a stand of its own for cooking on the ground, but if you have a flat-bottomed baking pot or large kettle, you will need a separate three-legged stand. The best ones are made from ordinary metal bar and consist of a triangle of steel with a leg at each corner. They have no fancy finishes as they spend their lives standing in the fire and provide a stable support for pots, pans and skottels. They're not height adjustable, so unless you push them deeper into the earth, the temperature has to be controlled by the amount of coals underneath.

Cast iron is not only used for making potjies, and there are attractive ranges of ovenware that can be used over an open fire. These large and small pots and casserole dishes are made the same way as a potjie, with clear, vitreous-enamel finishes. The lids are usually preformed steel plate with ovenproof handles.

Like the potjie they can be used to cook almost anything. They're slightly wider at the top than at the bottom, so are the ideal shape for making breads and cakes (which can simply be tipped out when done). Because they are flat-bottomed, when the fire is very hot they may need to be stood on something that keeps them off the coals. The handles are flat protrusions on either side and get as hot as the rest of the pot, so you will need two oven gloves or something similar to lift the pot off the fire. More sophisticated than a potjie in looks, the designs are simple, classic shapes.

THE SKOTTEL

A skottel (in its original form a discarded circular ploughshare) is another versatile item, and although you would find it difficult to make a stew in one, it can be used to cook just about anything else, from fried eggs to steak to stir-fried vegetables.

The modern skottel has an enamel finish and is often heated by gas. Those that can be used over an open fire are usually rectangular and made from steel plate with slightly raised sides and handles on each side (the corners are shaped like shallow spouts for pouring). The flat base means that food will not run towards the middle (as is the case with the round variety). Skottels make excellent 'warming trays' on the fire and form a natural surface for pancake-making.

CROCKERY AND UTENSILS

For hikers, lightness is usually the primary consideration. Tin billycans are light and extremely useful.

Dixies – those two deep square tins used by soldiers on manoeuvres – are still doing service, and can be used to cook in and eat out of. The larger one fits over the smaller one to form a strong metal box and the fold-out handles tuck neatly away.

Camping-utensil designers like the idea of everything fitting into everything else. You'll find many small cooking sets with one detachable handle that consist of a pan, two pots and a small kettle. They're usually made of aluminium, which has one of the highest strength-to-weight ratios of any metal, or very thin stainless steel. When packed up, the entire unit will fit into a space half the size of a shoebox.

Stainless steel survives outdoor use very well, and there is a huge variety of crockery available (much of it is an overflow from the professional catering industry). These pots, pans and other receptacles are hardwearing and although their mirror-like finish may fade with time, their resilience will not. Stainless steel is harder and therefore not as flexible as other metals, so even receptacles made from a thin-gauge plate will retain their shape, although some buckling may occur if left over a naked flame.

The range of utensils that can be used over an open fire is vast. A hand-made braai fork from the forge at a working museum (such as Kleinplasie outside Worcester in the Western Cape) is hard to beat in terms of individuality and atmosphere and can make a great gift – it may eventually even become a family heirloom. But stainless steel is undeniably the material of the age, and most commercially produced braai utensils are made from it.

Braai forks have largely been replaced by braai tongs and other implements (in a set of braai implements a long-handled basting brush is usually included). Tongs come in many different shapes and sizes – look out for the ones with scissor-like telescopic handles, which helpfully keep uncovered hands safe from the searing heat of the fire.

The 'flipping-over' tool is another ingenious device – it's a simple pointed hook bent at right angles to a long shaft. This allows the braaier to turn the meat over with a mere flick of the wrist. Picking pieces of meat up is just as easy.

THE OPEN FIRE

MAKING A FIRE

The first thing to do when preparing to make a fire is to find a suitable place. Most caravan parks have defined areas where you can do this, but few places are ideal all the time. Wind is fire's biggest enemy, and if you can avoid it by using your own portable braai, do so. The most erratic currents occur at ground level, so a good place to position your braai or make your fire would be in the lee of something large. Dense bushes form a natural windbreak, as do the crevices between large rocks. If the sheltered area is quite small, the fire needs to be made as close to the walls as possible so that any wind blows over the top. The area you want to protect is between the top of the coals and the underside of the grid.

If no suitable shelter is available and you are not camping on pristine lawn or loose sand, an easy option is to dig a hole in the ground. This will mean that your grid will end up at ground level, which might pose problems of its own – unless the ground is damp, do not build low walls with the earth you remove or with the first puff of wind any loose material will end up on your dinner. Tree trunks, logs, piles of stones or even branches with densely packed leaves – anything that disturbs the windflow – will help. The idea is to let the heat from the coals get to the grid unhindered and direct the smoke away from the party.

FIRE WOOD

The days where the camper or caravanner had to go out with an axe and look for fire wood are, to all intents and purposes, gone. With the impact that greater numbers of people are having on the environment, cutting down or breaking parts off a tree is either an offence or, at the very least, strongly discouraged. The breaking of anything, including trees, is an act of vandalism. Perpetrators can be blacklisted and banned from the venue in an effort to ensure a sustainable environment for everyone.

The good news is that fire wood will almost always be on sale at resorts, national parks and nature reserves. It is usually sold in strong plastic carry-bags with large holes on the sides. These hold the pieces together for ease of handling and allow moisture to escape. This does not mean that the wood will automatically be dry, though. At the end of a busy tourist season shop owners may sell wood that was cut down merely hours before. The telltale sign of wet wood is condensation under the plastic, which means that it must be left with the shop owner.

While there is no limit to how big you can make a fire, there does seem to be a minimum size for one that you intend cooking on, and it needs to consist of at least a few layers of dry wood. One piece of wood will burn with difficulty but four or five will give you a healthy blaze. Leave enough air between each piece for circulation. If packed too tightly, no air will be able to penetrate and the fire will go out or burn with difficulty. It's almost as if the fire needs to create its own updraught, which draws air in from the sides. No fire burns well without this natural convection.

Tip: If you have a crowd of starving children to feed who are nevertheless expecting a romantic fire, chop the wood into small pieces. Quartering a log about 6cm in diameter will give you a good, practical size.

How big a bed of coals you want is not always in proportion to the amount of wood you start out with. There needs to be enough of the right type of coals to prepare the meal for the whole party. Lighter woods such as pine burn too fast and may not make any coals at all. They can still be useful, as they are easy to chop up, splinter well and catch fire easily – this is what you need for getting a fire going if you don't have firelighters.

A wood fire will take time to burn down to the point where there are embers to cook on, as the flames produce temperatures that are far too high. When correctly controlled, small fires fed with twigs and sticks provide a better heat than coals if a big pan or skottel is being used. A large blaze will provide comforting warmth and light at night, but if you are planning to use the embers for cooking later, you may need an alternative light source like a torch or lantern to see what you are doing.

The larger the logs the longer they take to burn, and two or three can be kept burning all night if you keep pushing the burning ends together into the flames. Coals can be scooped out and placed nearby for cooking. Large dry logs will burn fast enough to supply you with coals all night if you feel that you may need them.

To cook meat you need a comparatively low heat – with no flames – that lasts for a long time. Hard woods make the best coals and there are several different types that vary in price depending on hardness and the scarcity of the resource. Kameeldoring from Namibia makes a truly fantastic fire (the grain can be so attractive that it seems a pity to burn it) but a small bundle can be almost double the price of other woods. Because the wood is very hard, the bigger pieces are difficult to chop up, and it burns for a long time before making coals. Rooikrantz and Black Wattle are quicker-growing and therefore softer, but they also make excellent coals that burn hot for a long time.

In wine-growing areas, off-cuts from the vineyards ('wingerdstokke' in Afrikaans), can be found at certain times of the year. They come in large packets, as the contorted shape of the vine stem makes packing more difficult. Because wingerdstokke have usually spent some time outside before being packed, they are usually quite dry and burn well. The pieces tend to be small and make good coals quickly.

If you are camping on a remote coastline, you may be tempted to collect driftwood – this may be prohibited, though, as driftwood forms part of the natural ecosystem and as it decays it provides food for smaller organisms to feed on.

One of the advantages of buying braai wood is that you know it will be safe to use. A surprising number of plants and trees are not fit for human consumption, and so strange plants you are unfamiliar with are best left alone, even if dried out.

In one famous case, a small party of travellers in Namibia made a fire from a dried-out Euphorbia (a large, tree-like cactus) and braaied their dinner over its coals. Euphorbia is a plant from which the San extracted the poison for their arrows, and using this for cooking can ruin a good braai! The diners all died before the could find help, and are buried where they braaied.

Most braai wood is 'purpose grown', so using it will have no adverse effect on some delicate ecosystem. Black Wattle is an alien species that grows very quickly and uses huge quantities of water. If left unchecked it becomes a threat to other plants and can choke riverbanks and streams, replacing less aggressive indigenous species – so it's a good idea to use it for fire wood.

COMPRESSED FUEL

The easiest – and dirtiest – fuel to use is charcoal, either natural charcoal or charcoal brickettes. Both come in 3kg or 5kg paper bags. Light them with a charcoal lighter, which is a large, thin metal tube, open at both ends and separated into two compartments about a third of the way up by a piece of expanded metal sheeting (braai grid). The larger top compartment holds a quantity of charcoal, and the smaller one covers the firelighters (or newspaper, or twigs). The tube keeps the heat concentrated in and around the charcoal, which ignites much quicker than if it had been standing in the open. Once lit, the tube is emptied and the charcoal spread out neatly under the grid.

The beauty of this method is that more charcoal can be added with very little bother, as and when necessary. A sturdy handle and heat deflector are attached to the side.

Fire packs are a relatively new idea, and contain all the elements needed to make a fire, except the matches or lighter. Packed the way you would assemble a normal wood fire, the packet it comes in takes the place of the firelighter. All you do is put the pack down where you want the fire to be and light it. This sets the fuel inside alight, and – in a short time – you have a fire.

There are other compressed fuels made from various combustible products that look something like large firelighters. They are convenient and at least one brand is made from pure wood. Yet, somehow, nothing beats the look, smell and general atmosphere of a natural wood or charcoal fire, and these remain the most popular options.

SAFETY

Making a fire can be great fun and add to the whole outdoor experience, but fire can also be a great destroyer. Leaving flames unattended or allowing fires to burn out of control can have devastating effects on the environment. Most wood fires produce showers of sparks from time to time, and these should not be allowed to come into contact with anything flammable, such as dry grass, tent fabric or clothing.

The speed at which dangerous situations develop is terrifying, especially if aided by wind. Large areas of dry grass are particularly susceptible and, once ignited, can become a natural blast furnace very quickly.

Runaway fires generate enormous amounts of heat, to the point where fire-fighters cannot even get close enough to the flames to put them out, and have to rely on other measures such as hastily dug firebreaks. This type of fire moves rapidly and threatens the life of any person or animal unfortunate enough to be caught in it: only the fleetest survive – usually only antelope, other large mammals and birds.

When you have finished with your fire, put it out completely so that there is no chance of it reigniting once you have gone. Pour plenty of water on the coals, or smother them with a generous amount of sand.

CHAPTER NINE

SLEEPING

WHAT TO SLEEP ON

In a caravan, you'll simply sleep in a bed. But for those who prefer the adventure of sleeping closer to Mother Earth – without sacrificing too much by way of comfort – there are a number of options.

Inflatable air mattresses come in single- or double-bed sizes. They hold a fair amount of air, so you will need some sort of pump to fill them (see chapter twelve). As they tend to be sturdy once inflated, they can usually be left that way. The top and bottom are kept in place with connecting strips inside, also determining the shape. Long-lasting under normal use, they are not designed to be used as a trampoline. If the inside strips tear loose, the mattress will develop shapeless parts and be expensive to repair. These mattresses are made from heavy rubberised fabric, making them fairly waterproof. Most have a slightly raised section to serve as a pillow, but this is no substitute for the real thing.

An important feature of air mattresses is the flat, or dimpled, upper and lower surfaces when inflated. It provides an even, flat surface on which to sleep. In cold weather a blanket on top of the mattress will provide extra insulation from below. Varying the air pressure will make for a harder or softer sleep.

Lilos can be used as mattresses, too, but they're not as robust and do not have a flat upper surface. The uneven tubular effect can be remedied to some extent by putting a folded blanket on top and releasing some air.

For hikers, small, high-density, roll-up foam mats are good value and make for efficient insulation from the cold earth, but they're not as comfortable as an air mattress.

Large pieces of ordinary foam provide a comfortable rest, if covered, but tend to take up a lot of space. If they get wet, they take a long time to dry. Hammocks are another option, but they can only be strung up outdoors and are not the most comfortable place to spend the night – which is a pity, as they are light and easy to carry. But don't leave your hammock behind – the upper, 'thin' end provides good head support, which is perfect for reading. In a cool breeze, the gentle rocking motion will quickly soothe you into a refreshing nap.

Because stretchers keep you off the ground, they offer good insulation. There is a wide selection of frames and fabric combinations out there, but the kinds to look for are small and light when folded up. Those with spring steel frames and legs that keep the sides apart will last for years.

One small drawback is that the feet tend to be narrower than the top, so do be careful when rolling over or you may tip yourself out. The wood and canvas ones may be very 'safari', but are quite heavy by comparison and not very rigid when up. If untreated canvas gets wet, it tends to stay that way until the sun comes out.

WHAT TO SLEEP IN

Sleeping bags are perhaps the most convenient form of bedding on earth, and even the most voluminous can be folded up into a relatively small package. No matter what the weather, you'll find a sleeping bag to match. They are graded according to the degree of insulation they provide against the cold: top of the range can cope with (literally) arctic conditions (-45°C), while lighter models are quite adequate for tropical regions.

In a discussion about sleeping bags, the terms 'inner', 'outer' and 'filling' may surface. These are the most important characteristics of a bag: what is the outside made from (is it waterproof?); what do you actually sleep in (does it have a cotton liner?); and what degree of insulation does the filling provide? A liner will keep the inside clean, and can be removed to sleep in on hot nights. A natural down-filling is one of the most efficient and will provide excellent insulation against the cold, but synthetic 'down' does not bunch together to form lumps and does not absorb moisture.

These are critical choices if you are venturing into a harsh and unforgiving environment, such as the icy slopes of a mountain. Do not hesitate if a good bag costs more than your tent, as under extreme conditions it can be a more important item. The lightest sleeping bags do not have to cope with much, and the most important decision may well be the design and colour of the fabric.

The quality of the zips is important for your choice of sleeping bag. If you're buying more than one, ask whether they can be zipped together to form a double.

Children's bags may be printed with cartoon characters and friendly wildlife scenes. Shortened bags are designed for very small children.

WHAT TO SLEEP UNDER

If you are caravanning, a sleeping bag may not be necessary. Consider the expense and the number of times you go away, and it might make more sense to use your bedding from home; this may mean extra washing, but at the well-equipped resorts this won't be a problem. When it gets really hot, you won't want to sleep under anything at all.

As long as you can seal off the sleeping area, insects should not become intrusive, and a mosquito net should only be necessary in extreme circumstances. To be 100 per cent effective, mosquito netting must be made from very fine gauze, which restricts airflow but is a whole lot better than getting malaria.

It is a good idea to bring your favourite pillow or cushion along. An extra bit of head and neck support can make all the difference.

CHAPTER TEN

CLOTHING

HEADGEAR

It's ironic that in eras gone by, when comparatively little was known about the harmful effects of the sun, hats were everyday wear. Today, however, it's still unusual to see people wearing sunhats unless they're on the beach.

The best hats for the harsh African sun have a full crown and a wide brim to keep the sun off your face and neck. An adjustable under-chin cord will keep your hat on in the wind and a fabric sweatband will absorb perspiration.

The most hardwearing fabric for hats is felt, but it's also one of the hotter and heavier fabrics – most felt safari-style hats (with zebra or mock-leopard skin hatbands) are aimed at image-conscious tourists. While they do have ventilation eyelets and an inner veil, these do not provide much airflow in very hot weather – and unless the sweatband is made of an absorptive material, it will not live up to its name. Such hats are, nevertheless, usually well styled and attractive and provide good protection from the elements.

Cricket hats, with their white uppers and green under the brim to reduce the glare, have proven their worth outdoors. In dusty environments they do tend to get soiled but are washed just as easily. As they're designed for active wear they tend to stay in place. The combination of firm brim and floppy crown is a winner, and the thin fabric is able to breathe easily.

Straw hats are not that long lasting, but they're cool and let lots of air circulate. Good air flow through the crown translates nicely into lowered wind resistance, which makes these another practical option.

Baseball caps may be very trendy – especially when worn backwards – but under a hot sun they provide little protection. Traditional European hats do not fare well in Africa, and you would do better to wear a traditional conical Xhosa or Basotho hat than a flat English cap or deerstalker. The Panama hat, designed in and for the tropics, works well for most lovers of outdoor life, but it is somewhat refined and looks better worn with a white linen suit than with khaki shorts and sandals.

JACKETS AND JERSEYS

The most popular jacket among campers is the nylon windbreaker with a drawstring at the hood and waist, elasticised wrists and a white towelling lining. They are machine washable and come in several attractive colours. Most are showerproof if not actually waterproof, and offer excellent protection against the wind without being too hot.

For high altitudes, a good padded jacket made from Ventex or Goretex is ideal. Both materials are quite waterproof yet the weave allows the jacket to breathe and so avoid annoying condensation. The hoods are usually double layered and fold up into the collar, with a zip or Velcro to keep them in place. (If the hood is too thin, there should be space for a warm balaclava to be worn underneath.)

European-style waxed jackets made from natural fibres (and usually in natural colours) are quieter than the artificial fabrics, which is important if you want to get close to game. They also do not produce the static associated with synthetics.

Voluminous ponchos may be great for rain forests but they restrict arm movement, so you do not see many of them around. A good waterproof jacket should be adequate in a relatively dry country such as South Africa – as long as you do not plan to rely on it for long periods in extravagant downpours.

SHIRTS, PANTS, SOCKS AND SHOES

Camp-style clothing should be hardwearing and in a colour that disguises dirt. Fabrics that are easy to wash, quick drying and don't need ironing are the way to go. They need to be quite colour-fast, though, especially if you plan to use a laundrette where the sorting is done by others.

CLOTHING

Shirts with long sleeves (they can be rolled up if it gets too hot) will protect your arms from the sun while you're driving. Buy them in a light, summery fabric such as polyester/cotton. Big collars can be folded up to protect your neck in the angled late-afternoon sun.

A pair of light-fabric trousers will also protect against the sun's deadly rays during the day and stinging insects in the evenings.

Shorts with elasticised waists, deep pockets and wild patterns seem to be a successful formula. If you can swim in them as well, so much the better.

Hikers will already know that good, thick socks not only save your feet but provide an airspace between foot and shoe that keeps feet cooler than if you were wearing thinner socks with a tighter weave. Ordinary socks are fine for everyday use, but can be the cause of painful blisters if you are planning extensive walks.

Shoes and sandals should be hardwearing. Many adverts imply that the two are interchangeable, but this is not always true. Good-quality sandals can be worn just about anywhere, but shoes provide 'sideways safety' – they protect your feet from thorns and other sharp objects that may damage the sides of your feet and they stop small sharp objects from getting between your foot and the sole of your shoe, or between your toes. Ankle boots provide extra support and protection, but in either case good-quality design and materials is a minimum requirement if you want them to survive extended outdoor use.

WINTER CLOTHING

There are whole ranges of specialised clothing designed for use in very cold climates. While most South Africans will never need them, it is good to know they exist. But do bear in mind that cold is a bigger enemy than heat, and greater precautions need to be taken if you are venturing into remote, cold-weather areas.

SUNGLASSES

Sunglasses need to protect your retina from ultra-violet rays, so look out for a sticker noting the UV rating somewhere on the lens. Buy the pair with the maximum rating.

Frames should be light but strong, and the latest (and most

expensive) material is Titanium. Great care should be taken when choosing the lenses, though. The better the quality of the glass lens, the sharper the picture will be, and with a good pair you should detect no deterioration of visual picture. Do also investigate the newest sport sunglasses, made from splinter-proof plastics.

If you already wear glasses, you may want to have them coated with UV-resistant layer. This light-sensitive material darkens when exposed to sunlight, but is almost transparent when you are in the shade again. Depending on how dark you want them to go, you can have more than one coating added. Three coats would do quite dark, although not as dark as ordinary sunglasses.

Do not neglect your children's eyes! If you meet with any resistance to sunglasses, explain that 'shades' are, in fact, a fashion statement. Special elastic bands will keep them on barely there nose bridges, and brightly coloured 'safety lines' will stop them from falling onto the ground and getting stood on.

CHAPTER ELEVEN

STORAGE

CLOTHING

In a caravan there's usually plenty of storage place – the problem is deciding what to leave behind. But don't leave behind your plastic laundry basket, especially if you are going to do a lot of hiking or have a small family and need to launder clothing every day. The basket can always be used to keep things from falling about while you're travelling.

Plastic hangers are a good choice, as they can be left permanently in the caravan and won't attract mildew. They are light and can be bought in packs of 10 or 20.

In a tent, collapsible cupboards are a great way to organise clothing. A small unit will take only a few minutes to assemble. The structure comprises a dismantleable treated metal frame covered in plastic, with a zip instead of a door. The larger ones have plenty of hanging space.

Clothes survive better if they are kept on hangers, as the weight of the garment pulls the fabric along the natural lines of the drape. (Ironing may make a garment look better but it shortens its life at the same time – the best argument against the chore of ironing clothes on holiday!)

Don't hang up jerseys and other knitted items as they'll lose their shape. Rather fold them on a shelf with socks and underwear.

Cardboard boxes are rigid and strong enough to last for the duration of the average holiday, and stacked on their sides, one on top of the other, they keep items neatly visible in a throw-away version of a modern modular display shelf. If you want to pack up your tent and move, simply fold the boxes flat.

Black refuse or green garden bags are the lightest, most convenient

LIMIT YOUR WEIGHT

To limit the number of things you take with you and to keep the weight/volume distribution fair, pretend you're loading an aeroplane and stipulate how many kilos are allowed per passenger. This should be a realistic amount so that no essential items get left at home. In a family, there may be certain bags that contain general items, and these need to be added to the overall weight. Each person is then allowed one bag into which everything has to fit – this allows for a certain amount of personal choice but keeps volumes practical.

way in which to transport clothing. They are strong enough to hold many clothes and, as long as each item is neatly folded and packed flat, the minimum of crumpling and folding will occur. A full bag of clothing packed this way can be carefully fitted into almost any space, where other more rigid items cannot go. They can be used inside the storage bins of caravans and motorhomes as well, and when taped or tied shut will keep dust from entering.

There is a wide range of travel bags made from combinations of synthetic fabrics. Their strong zips with double-lockable travellers and large, padded handles make them ideal for campers. The ones to look out for have several smaller compartments on the outside of a large central one, which means that things don't get mixed up and everything is accessible. Although they are designed for transporting clothing and personal effects, they are well suited to storing them too.

Suitcases do a passable job, but their rigid shape is not easy to accommodate when you're trying to fit everything into your already overcrowded boot. Rather have several small, soft bags.

Backpacks are a great place in which to store things. They are strong and survive the rigours of travel well – that's what they've been designed to do. But if you're planning to do a lot of hiking and walking, you'll need some other method of storage, too, or you'll spend too much time packing and unpacking. When packing, prioritise items for easy grabbing. The large backpacks are rather deep, which is a nuisance if you need something that is at the bottom.

Tin trunks are worth considering if you're going off-road and need something that can take the punishment meted out by miles of uneven roads; they're also lockable. They may end up with a few dings, but they're difficult to break. The seams are spot-welded – the layers of metal have been melted together. To break them open you would literally have to 'unmelt' them, and this is way beyond the scope of the ordinary roadside pilferer.

For extra security make sure you have a good strong lock that cannot be broken easily. A laminated body or stainless-steel casing is best. Trunks have strong metal handles, which, apart from making them a lot easier to pick up, also allow you to chain them to a tree, your roof rack or the top of your trailer.

TOILETRIES

It may sound like a good idea to keep all the toiletries together in one bag 'so they don't get lost', but it is more likely that 'when they get lost the whole lot will go'. Rather let everyone pack their own, even if it means going on holiday with several tubes of toothpaste and bars of soap. The small and cheap zip-up washbags are fine and, as they will be used for only a few weeks a year, they will last a surprisingly long time.

FOOD

DRY FOODS

The smaller collapsible cupboards that consist of shelf space only are as good for storing canned and dry foods as they are for storing clothes. The same goes for cardboard boxes, and these can be used in the usual way, opening side up.

WET FOODS

If you do not have a fridge or freezer, keep perishables such as milk, meat etc. in a cooler box. If you keep buying ice, you should be able to keep the temperature acceptably low. Pickling or marinating meat was an effective method of preservation before the advent of the freezer: vacuum pack the whole mixture in strong plastic bags (you can buy your own machine that does this) and keep it cool – it will not only last longer but will taste better as well. Vacuum sealable containers are particularly efficient if you exclude as much air as possible.

It is also a good idea to deep-freeze items before leaving, as it is much easier to keep the temperature down than it is to get it there in the first place.

Flasks can be used to keep food warm or cold for up to eight hours – a wide-mouthed version is good for stews, for example. Fill the container to the maximum and the contents will hold their temperature longer. If hot enough, the final stages of cooking can take place in a flask. The secret to keeping things hot in flasks is to exclude as much air as possible.

WATER

In a relatively dry country such as ours, we need to carry water wherever we travel.

If it's for the radiator, any sturdy, clean container will do – the metal jerry can is an off-road favourite. Take more care with containers for drinking water, as the contents must remain fresh. Strong Polythene containers of various sizes are the lightest and the most popular, and as they're white and semi-opaque, you can see how full they are. They come in many shapes and sizes, from 1 litre to 25 litres, and you can usually buy tap attachments for the larger ones.

Hiking-style water bottles hold only a litre or so. Run the carrying strap through the handle of an enamel mug if it is for communal use. Try to find a bottle with good insulation, to keep the water pleasantly cool. If you intend adding minerals or flavourings, remember that certain plastics absorb the taste and/or smell more or less permanently – rather let this happen in the cup and not the bottle.

The larger insulated water containers are justifiably popular. Go for the best you can afford, as the cheap give very short notice when they fail. Breather holes and spring-loaded valves should be easy to open and the flow should be positive. If it isn't, suspect a blockage or poor design.

Throwing a handful of ice blocks in before putting on the top provides relief when you need it most. Or pour about 1,5 litres of water into a well-rinsed 2-litre plastic cold-drink container and place it in the freezer (with the bottle lying on its side). Just before leaving, fill it with tap water. You should now have cold water for many hours and can keep filling it till the ice melts completely, which takes a long time.

Stand liquid containers in cardboard boxes and pack things like dishcloths and hand towels around them to stop them from falling over. When travelling, vibration can work the tops loose, but as long as they don't fall over, damage will be minimised. Pack containers where they are easy to reach, and if you are changing altitude, release pressure by opening and closing airtight lids when you stop to refuel.

Canvas containers keep water cool and fresh-tasting. The larger types, which look like a big, square box with an opening at the bottom front, have a compartment under the water tank that makes for a convenient miniature cool room; it is possible to store perishables quite safely in such a system, even in the hottest weather.

The containers drip quite a lot at first and require regular filling in the beginning, but after 24 hours the canvas swells to the point where it allows only the evaporation necessary for heat dispersion.

FUEL AND DISTILLATES

Fuel is normally carried in metal jerry cans as these are well tried and have a proven track record in the harshest of conditions. They can be locked or wired shut, and a simple but sturdy rubber seal keeps the contents free from pollutants – such as dust. Apart from their strength, the main advantage of a jerry can is its large volume, which is just the right size to remain easily portable.

Paraffin and other fuels like alcohol or Benzine need smaller but no less sturdy containers. Metal can take the most punishment, but good-quality plastics are a close second. A screw-on or lever-assisted lid is preferable but a strong seal is essential.

CHAPTER TWELVE

ACCESSORIES

Accessories – or 'extras', 'options', 'non-essentials' or pure luxuries – improve either the enjoyment or the efficiency of a particular activity or item. The range and variety is astonishing – as are some of the prices. And what is a luxury will, of course, depend to a large extent on what you are used to. Genuine down sleeping bags, for example, may be considered luxuries only under certain conditions.

Price is often the deciding factor when it comes to accessories – and what you are prepared to pay has a great influence on the price!

So take your time, consider each item and don't buy anything that does not have some real use – that way you'll amass a collection of useful equipment that will continue to give you pleasure long after you've finished paying for it.

PROTECTION FROM THE ELEMENTS

Sun umbrellas come in more sizes and fabric varieties than ever before – with dark wood and cream-coloured canvas guaranteeing a 'safari' look. Along with quality and price comes longevity, and how important this is depends on how often you are going to use it.

The smallest ones are easy to carry, but you're not able to angle the head on all models. If they're made from light-gauge metal they may suffer damage when being hammered or forced into a standing position in the sand. Another accessory will solve this problem: a sturdy metal umbrella stand that is hammered into the ground instead.

The biggest umbrellas are difficult to carry and need their own stands.

If you are short handed or catering for a particularly large group, consider buying a lightweight gazebo of the pavement-stall style. They require a lot more putting up than do umbrellas, but are less likely to blow away in the wind because of their large, rigid frames. The largest ones have sides that do a wonderful job of protecting occupants from the slanting rays of the afternoon sun. Once up, it is a simple job to move them around or turn them to a more convenient angle.

As long as you never feel the need to stand up and stretch, a cup-shaped wind shelter is an excellent accessory. They are very light and look almost like small dome tents with one side missing; they even work as an outdoor sleeping shelter. They collapse into an easy-to-carry pack that is smaller than a folded beach umbrella, and a few light pegs keep them from blowing away. Many have sewn-in ground sheets.

Windbreaks may sound a bit extravagant and somewhat unnecessary, but are nevertheless popular among campers who spend a few weeks at a time in one place. The largest consist of a loose-weave fabric stretched between a series of poles that remains upright with guy ropes and pegs. They provide privacy and superior shelter from wind.

TABLES AND CHAIRS

Fold-up tables may seem like a luxury at first, especially if you own a large, well-equipped caravan with an inside dining area. But if a lot of cooking is going to be done outdoors, or if the temperature is simply going to make eating indoors unpleasant, a good fold-up table will make a tangible difference to the day-to-day pleasures of living and eating outdoors.

A fold-up table and chair unit with four bench seats and place for an umbrella is a great thing to have, especially if you're camping in a tent with small children. The chairs cannot fall over, be rocked on or moved at all, which keeps the smaller family members feeling secure and gives the parents that little extra peace of mind. They can be folded up quickly and easily, and their handles enable them to be carried like a suitcase (great to take with on picnics and day trips).

The range of fold-up chairs is vast. Metal frames with canvas are heavier but stronger than plastic or wood, and are well suited to real bush or wilderness use. Wooden ones are heavier, and when folded up are not as compact, but if you feel it's important to create the right atmosphere, the warm grain and satin finish of hand-oiled wood is hard to beat.

Clean white plastic tubing with synthetic coverings is very practical and continues to be one of the most popular options. Wooden deck chairs are among the most comfortable for reclining, but are impossible for positioning at a table (and are very difficult to eat in!). On the beach, however, they are in a class of their own.

BRAAI UNITS

Portable braais are becoming more popular among travellers as the designs become more sophisticated and the products lighter and more efficient. Kettle braais are a good example as they are lightweight and long lasting. They come in a wide range of manageable sizes and can be used to make a wide variety of foods. With the lid on, the air flow can be finely tuned and they are mercifully easy to clean. More important, they contain heat well and are considered a perfectly safe place to make a fire when there are non-permanent places available. Their ideal fuel is compressed charcoal brikettes, which are light and conveniently packaged.

Fold-up, stainless-steel plate braais are expensive but, when well made, are good value for money. They're made to be light and easy to transport, so even the larger ones can hold only enough food to feed a family. Conventional braais are popular among those who still like to make a wood fire. The range here is even more vast, and can be viewed everywhere from well-established hardware chain stores to stalls at car-boot sales. Small businesses often rely on greater flexibility to survive, and if you want something specific, it is more than likely they can make it up for you. You may even wish to make your own, highly personalised model. The satisfaction that comes from braaiing in something you have spent many hours making yourself is beyond compare. Do remember, though, that weight is important, so the finished product must be strong, but not too heavy.

There is a truly astounding variety of braai tools and they make great gifts – buy them from almost anywhere, from upmarket decor stores to corner cafés. And this is another area in which the DIYer can excel. The designs are fairly simple, so good tools can easily be constructed from off-cut black metal bar bought at scrap yards or found in the waste bins at metal merchants. Stainless steel is difficult to weld, while mild steel can be heated and bent to shape. To stop the latter from rusting, bring it to a low heat and paint with a light covering of boiled linseed oil.

Good oven or braai gloves cost little but save much. A burnt hand can remain painful for many hours and ruin a good evening. First prize is not to get burnt at all, so choose a pair with enough insulation. Welding gloves work just as well and the more professional ones have sleeves that go up to your elbows. If you do happen to get the inside of your fingers burned, keep an ice-cold can of beer in your hand – it'll do much to ease the pain. When the contents start to warm up, which they do after a short while, just put it back in the cool box and get out a new one. Depending on the severity of the burn, you may need to 'recycle' quite a few.

OTHER ACCESSORIES

If you are going off the beaten track or simply wish to make use of an abundant source of free energy, consider a solar shower. They are very efficient as long as there is enough sun to warm up the water. Hunters on remote safaris make good use of them where their morale-boosting qualities are greatly appreciated.

Small, hand-operated washing machines are the solution to having to wash clothes by hand. They are very efficient, reasonably priced and will clean a great many clothes with a minimum of effort. When the drum is filled with hot water, it becomes slightly pressurised, and because the lid forms a tight seal the only place for the pressure to go is into the fibres. A few turns of the handle and the washing is done. The only remaining questions: do you have the space and the money? Portable washing lines are especially useful if you are camping out in the bush, where the only alternative is thorn bushes.

If you go camping often, consider a separate ground sheet, which will prolong the life of your tent floor. But if you're backpacking in the mountains and pitch your tent on dense grass each night, they're hardly worth considering.

Flasks are great for family use and their popularity can be judged by the number of large companies that make them. The best ones are not necessarily the most expensive, and you should check to see what spare parts are available as you will be keeping it for some time.

It's always great to have hot toast for breakfast, and you can buy a handy toaster that will work over your gas stove or hot coals. One of the most efficient makes is also the simplest and consists of a small piece of fine-gauge expanded metal sheeting held in a square metal plate with the sides turned up to hold it in. These hold four slices of bread, which are toasted one side at a time. They work well but get very hot, so be extra careful when removing them from the heat source.

A good cooler box can be expensive but if you consider the amount of use it is likely to see over a period of years, the price becomes almost immaterial. Buy one with the best-possible insulation – try to get hold of a product test conducted by a reputable company before making up your mind. Polystyrene is not the hardiest material but is it one of the better insulators. Cooler boxes made from this are the lightest by far. The secret is to pack the most critical food items at the bottom, where the air is coldest. Keep them cool with reusable freezer packs or packets of ice.

Glass and can-holders that keep drinks off the ground might look somewhat frivolous but they do a wonderful job of keeping grass and sand out of that long-awaited beer or juice. Insulated, plastic can or bottle holders work well in keeping the temperature down and some can even be worn around your neck to make sure you always know the whereabouts of your beer. A wet cloth just doesn't keep wine or beer cold quite as well!

And one last accessory: a spring balance or bathroom scale. Before packing the car, caravan or trailer, weigh the bigger items and jot down the results. It only takes seconds! Once you know what everything weighs, packing goes that much more quickly. When it comes to balancing your car and caravan or trailer, use a bathroom scale to find out how much weight is pushing down on your towbar. Lift up the jockey wheel of the caravan (or the foot of the trailer) and lower it onto the scale. It should not read more than 90kg for a caravan and about 35–45kg for a trailer, depending on its size.

CHAPTER THIRTEEN

CAMPING WITH CHILDREN

Camping is one of childhood's greatest adventures, and the times you spend with your children having fun in a tent or caravan will remain in their memories forever and unite your family in later years.

The sheer novelty of it all and the fact that the whole world comes so much closer may have something to do with this. Whatever the reason, don't hesitate when it comes to packing them into the car and going away.

Children take to camping like the proverbial duck to water, and apart from when fatigue overtakes them, the simplest pleasures still have the ability to carry them further, and in a more wholesome fashion, than the most expensive toys.

BEFORE YOU LEAVE HOME

If small children are feeling insecure about leaving home, they instinctively recognise their role as the 'unfortunate' in need of attention. A familiar toy can be very comforting, and if you explain that 'we' are taking teddy (or rabbit or frog) on holiday, their attention is not only diverted but their sense of insecurity is transferred to the toy: they become the comforter and their toy the comforted, and you may have peace for another 15 minutes.

By the time you get behind the wheel to leave, you may just be a little tired yourself, and the last thing you need is to try to run a playschool while driving hundreds of kilometres. Not to say you will

KEEPING YOUR COOL

In very hot weather, ice blocks or freezer packs wrapped in a face cloth keep children cool and are fun to hold. As the ice blocks melt they may change into weird and wonderful shapes. Encourage caution as the blocks get smaller, although in hot weather they won't stay that way for long. Flavoured drinks frozen into ice blocks are even better and are thirst quenching as well.

never have to do this – but the idea is to prevent it at all costs. Don't be disappointed if life does not come out perfectly – a philosophical attitude can be a valuable asset in keeping your edges from getting frayed. If you have small children and manage to get life going even half according to plan, you're doing very well indeed.

I know it's aiming high, but try to coincide your departure, travel or arrival times with natural sleep patterns; this can make life a lot easier for both parent and child. Even if you get it right for just the first half hour or a stint between towns, you will have lessened the strain to some extent. The hum of the engine and the warmth of the car have a natural tranquillising effect, and if it's nap time anyway, you can be guaranteed at least one spell of peace and quiet so you can concentrate on the road. Be warned: like other rhythm methods it's not foolproof – but at least if it goes wrong the results are not so serious!

ON THE ROAD

Transform the back of the car into a 'special' place with blankets and pillows. Explain to your children that this is being done for their enjoyment and they will learn from an early age that holidaying is a time when everyone has great fun. Remember that they may have no previous experience to rely on and will believe (almost) everything you tell them. It's true that it's always safer to travel with your child

PAY ATTENTION

No parent can ignore a troubled child, and even though there may be two parents in the car, the distraction value for the parent behind the wheel remains high – and herein lies the danger. The cause of many an accident happens in a split second as the driver's attention wavers. If both parents' attention is required, rather find a safe place and pull over. Apart from being much safer, doing what needs to be done can be handled more quickly that way.

strapped in, but show me a child who can remain this way for hours on end ...

Keep a good food supply handy to lessen the need for disruption on the journey, and a quick snack can be quite absorbing. A nice chunk of salty biltong will keep teething babies happy (for a while). Biltong is easy for small hands to grip and most children love the taste. Babies end up sucking it or getting only tiny bits off at a time, so the danger of choking is minimal and it lasts and lasts and lasts! Do not buy pieces that are too dry, though, as they can be sharp on soft little mouths.

For slightly older children the passing scenery is often a source of fascination, although you may have to keep reminding them that this is so. Stop the car every now and then and get out and look around. There are always things to see on the way, be it interesting rock formations, unusual activities (like strange-looking machines driving up and down in a field) or cows, sheep or ostriches in pens next to the road. Prop up your tiny passengers with cushions so that they can have a good view while the car is moving, and if they are old enough and you can arm them with a pair of binoculars, so much the better.

Slow down as you go past hawks and other raptors perched on power lines or telegraph poles. As long as you stay in the car they will let you get amazingly close, and binoculars will make it look like they are sitting on your arm. The binoculars turned the wrong way will also make mum look like she's on the horizon, which is the source of much hilarity. (They say it's all about discovery.)

Children can be highly competitive, and coping with this will require a firm and decisive hand. If, like many families, you have only one of some highly sought-after object (like a pair of binoculars), make sure that everyone gets equal time with it. Allocate a certain number of minutes per person, and stick to it. Cooler boxes (no pun intended) are good for creating barriers between squabbling children, although in a perfect world, of course, they would simply obey every parental command.

Small towns are fun to stop at and often have interesting museums or historical monuments. Because of their size these may not merit more than half an hour at the most, but any break from the monotony of driving should be welcomed, even if it's a quick swim in a public pool or a 10-minute stroll along a river bank. For children brought up in a city, even miles and miles of open space can be quite awe-inspiring.

Natural family hierarchy dictates that parents sit in the front seats of the car. Only as a special treat and for limited time are junior members of the tribe allowed into the hallowed ground. There is no real benefit to sitting in front, and the back seats are often more comfortable, as they have higher backs and provide more freedom of movement. Even so, it's amazing how seriously this seating is taken. A few hours 'out of your environment' can have huge novelty value and, ridiculous though it may sound, provide a refreshing change. Do be warned, though, that you will be lowering your 'status' by doing this and will become subject to the 'street laws' that prevail in the back of the car.

FEARS AND DANGERS

Once you have arrived at your destination, check out the surrounding area for anything that might constitute a danger to your child. This can be anything from a communal braai area where hot coals are still burning to a large nest of biting ants. A nearby pool full of happy children is irresistible to any toddler, who may simply wander off to see what's

IT'S A COVER-UP

Protecting sensitive young skin from the sun is very important, especially in Africa, so take extra care when you and your children spend time outdoors. Sunscreen, protective clothing, hats and a sensible attitude towards the sun will pay off in the long run. Children tend to play until they start feeling uncomfortable, by which time it's probably too late. Assume maximum exposure and cover them accordingly.

---

going on. Other children who may not have smaller siblings can cause unintentional trauma, and accidents happen quickly. Small boys racing around on bicycles may not notice a child in their path until it's too late. If you see a dangerous situation developing, shout loudly to attract their attention!

Children's fear of the dark can be turned around with a few cheap torches, which they can use to shine into nooks and crannies as it gets dark. Many insects come out only at night, and are not as aggressive as during the day. (The exception is mosquitoes. If there are many of these about, cover liberally with an appropriate insect repellent.) For daytime fun, make sure you have buckets, spades and nets: small crustaceans are great fun in a bucket of water, although do be careful of the ones that can nip.

Most of South Africa's resorts are close to rural areas, where there is the strong possibility of contact with wild animals. These do not have to be the big five. Monkeys and baboons are extremely agile and can move with alarming speed, which can frighten – if not harm – you or your child. Primates can be daring, especially those that have overcome their fear of humans. An encounter with an aggressive animal wrenching food out of his or her hands can be the cause of nightmares and fears for years to come. Even large – and harmless – insects such as locusts can give everyone a fright.

When it comes to mud and water, children will play happily for hours on end. You do not want to curtail this wonderful activity, so if there is deeper water nearby, make sure they have well-fitting and well-tried flotation devices that are life preservers as well. You still need to be with them all the time, but the better devices do allow a broader aquatic experience and make them feel more secure. And they're great fun.

Rivers and estuaries can be dangerous places. Many of them carry water with a visibility close to zero, and anyone who cannot swim will find themselves in serious trouble very quickly. Struggling children do not produce much turbulence when under water, and if the current is strong there may be no sign of the victim's whereabouts. The rule is, fortunately, very simple: never take your eyes off your children when they're playing in or near water – not even for a second. Leave the book or magazine at home – the peace of mind you get from having your child safely in sight will more than make up for it.

The seaside can also be particularly treacherous, with waves and undercurrents coming as if from nowhere. No matter how benign conditions may seem and how many other people are around, do not let anyone in out of their depth, and be prepared to move quickly if you need to.

The same applies when walking or hiking in unfamiliar territory. Do not allow your children out of your sight. Few pathways are signposted as being potentially dangerous, but a step just slightly too much to one side can have unpleasant consequences. A short lecture before setting off may make the difference between safe and sorry. Do not make it sound like a threat, though – make a point of telling your children that it's because you care about them!

CHAPTER FOURTEEN

SURVIVAL

It's a typical, light-hearted question asked by colleagues and friends on your return from a holiday undermines the importance of survival: 'So, how well did you survive?' It is true that even the remoter trails are laid-out with pleasure and relaxation in mind, and unless you ignore sane advice you should not have to rely on genuine survival skills to get back home. But there are still many ways in which the ignorant and the unsuspecting can get into trouble.

SNAKES

Snakes occur throughout the country, and it is worth knowing that Africa is home to the greatest variety of venomous snakes on earth. These simple and misunderstood creatures should always be treated with respect (approximately 5m is usually enough).

Many are certainly dangerous to humans, but it is a little-known fact that because they extract their protein from venom, they may bite but not inject the victim, if they can possibly get away with it. There are three types of venom, and treating a bite effectively means being able to positively identify the species and ascertain whether there was venom injected or whether it was a 'dry', warning bite. Isolating the bite with a tourniquet is not the lifesaver it was considered years ago, even if it is clear you have received a full bite.

If you are going to a remote area where there is a real risk of being bitten by one of the more dangerous species, read up thoroughly on the ones you are likely to encounter and make sure you take the necessary precautions and anti-venom.

Snakes are very sensitive to vibration, and if you are walking heavily, you will alert them to your presence and they may move off. Puff-adders, though, are ponderous and slow-moving, and tend to go into 'red-alert' mode sooner than do other snakes as they wait for you to pass. They are erectile-fanged, which means that their fangs fold out and point slightly forward when striking, which they do with alarming speed. They are responsible for about 80 per cent of fatal snake bites in Africa.

Incorrect treatment can aggravate a situation, so if and when the time comes, remain calm and place things in proper perspective. Some years ago a couple travelling in Namibia stopped to repair a vehicle. While he was under the car, the husband was bitten by a snake seeking shade. They both panicked, and the wife injected a full ampoule of anti-venom into her husband's stomach. She pushed the needle of a second syringe-full right through his shin and the contents of the ampoule sprayed onto the tar.

At the nearest hospital, the husband was treated for an internal haemorrhage caused by his over-enthusiastic wife, and the snake (which was probably bludgeoned to death) turned out to be absolutely harmless!

Hikers in hot, rocky places may feel better-equipped taking along a snake-bite kit, but the anti-venom has a limited shelf life, even under ideal conditions (which are unlikely to exist in your backpack). Rather avoid getting bitten in the first place: with a few exceptions, most snakes only react to movement – so during an encounter, try to stay motionless. Given the opportunity, most snakes would rather escape than risk injury in a confrontation, and after a few minutes will slide cautiously away.

There have been isolated reports of snake-bite victims being treated with stun guns (but this has not been scientifically researched!). When no other treatment methods were available, wires were attached to the electrodes of the stun gun and the loose ends pushed gently into the puncture holes made by the fangs. The ensuing charge of high-voltage electricity reportedly reversed the effects of the venom. After recovering from the initial shock, victims reported feeling better in as little as 10 or 15 minutes, and rescuers reported reduced swelling of the bite area.

MALARIA

Malaria seems to be on the increase and the effectiveness of the treatment on the decrease. Locals, who cannot live on a constant diet of pills, rely on other forms of prevention.

Malaria is an illness that stays with the victim for many years, so do not take chances when going to infested areas. Many otherwise careful travellers fall prey to mosquito bites around party time, when they suffer from impaired judgement brought on by too much alcohol. Mosquito nets are a good preventative measure at night, as they keep other creepy crawlies out as well. Coils will repel all insects but should not be relied on for avoiding a dose of malaria. Be careful not to breath in the smoke of the poisonous smouldering coils; they should not be burnt in enclosed spaces as the toxins can concentrate in a restricted atmosphere.

Daytime is another matter altogether, and you can rely on the wide variety of wipe-on, smear-on, dab-on preparations to keep you from being bitten. Varying rates of success get reported with many of these products. Remember if it's hot and you are perspiring a lot, you need several applications to maintain the levels at an effective concentration.

Mosquitoes are more aggressive at night, so during early morning or around sundown, change into a top with long sleeves, trousers that cover your ankles and a windbreaker with a light hood that covers your neck and ears. Make a habit of covering remaining bits of exposed skin with the previously mentioned treatments and you will have gone a long way to ensuring you survive your bush adventure without discomfort.

Consult your doctor before deciding which prophylactic pills to take, and ask whether this is the latest and most effective method.

STINGS AND BITES

Preparations such as Stingoes offer immediate relief, although several applications may be necessary before the symptoms disappear completely. These preparations are good to have around and do not take up much space in your medical kit. For more serious bites from scorpions or spiders, get the patient to medical attention as soon as you can. Severity of symptoms can often be related to body weight, so the condition of small children and the elderly should always be treated with urgency.

POISONOUS PLANTS

A surprising number of plants are poisonous when ingested, and some can inflict pain or severe discomfort if you so much as brush against their leaves or stems. Nettles are one such example, and on Table Mountain the blister bush can leave you with an unpleasant reminder of a close encounter. Learn what the plants look like, so you can apply the correct remedy or avoid contact with them altogether. (Whether or not to induce vomiting, for example, depends on the type of plant, and there is really no shortcut to knowing which plant you are dealing with.)

SHELLFISH

Beware of ingesting crustaceans if there has been a 'red tide'. 'Red tide' is a poisonous form of plankton found floating in large patches at sea, and is one of the natural foods of mussels and other filter-feeders. Eating mussels that have fed on these plankton can be fatal. Initial symptoms are nausea and numbness of the lips and mouth.

Filter-feeders such as mussels and periwinkles remain poisonous for some time after feeding on the plankton, so if you are planning on collecting your own, find out from local authorities when the last red tide was. If you can't get a satisfactory answer, play it safe by not eating any at all.

YOUR EMERGENCY BOX

Thick, strong sticking plaster .with powerful adhesive qualities should accompany you everywhere, but make sure you have some form of gauze to stop it sticking to the wound itself. Always carry a pair of sharp scissors or knife to cut it with, as it is almost impossible to tear. The stickiest plaster does not usually allow much air to penetrate, so you may also wish to carry a different variety that does.

Bandages can be used to stop bleeding, pack an open wound or immobilise a broken limb by tying it to a splint. Sprained ankles can also be effectively bound, and you can even use bandages as a filter to strain plant matter from water. Rolled lengths of elasticised bandage are the most common, and are obtainable at most good pharmacies. They are cheap and weigh very little, so every medical kit should have at least one. A triangular bandage on its own would provide better support for immobilising a broken arm, especially if no splint can be found, although the rolled elasticised one is probably more versatile.

Painkillers are good for minor discomforts, and some of these, such as heat and eyestrain, are often the cause of headaches. The pills are light enough for you to take along different types of varying strengths. And potent anti-histamines can make life more bearable for sinus and asthma sufferers.

Good eye-drops will provide welcome relief for sore eyes (and will make you look better). A set of tweezers (make sure they close precisely at the ends) will allow you to remove the smallest of thorns or spines; prickly pears are the worst offenders here, and if someone gets one of these tiny thorns in their lips or tongue, they will be glad you brought a good magnifying glass. This handy instrument can be used for lighting fires in an emergency as well.

For less serious discomforts, there is a host of remedies. The anti-septic cream Zambuk, for example, has a wide range of applications, including temporary lubrication of squeaky mountain bike chains. Vaseline or lip-ice will prevent chapped, sore lips and soothe cracked, dry skin.

If you're hiking, always carry a supply of energy bars and/or chocolate. Chocolate melts in hot weather, but it can still be eaten with a spoon – and it is excellent for morale.

Sticks of biltong saw tens of thousands of Boer soldiers through the war, and 100 years later this dried-meat snack is still a good form of energy and can last for weeks or even months without losing its flavour. You may need a good knife to cut it (but this you should have, anyway) and a stone to keep the knife sharp. Cutting biltong into thin slivers makes it easier to chew, and although you can buy it that way in packets, cutting it up yourself is a lot more fun – a bit like filling a pipe with tobacco.

Hikers tend to wander further away from help than do most people. A small metal mirror for signalling and a spare pair of bootlaces should go with you everywhere and don't take up too much space. You'll find no substitutes for either of them in the veld, and a loose hiking boot can chafe or blister your feet to the point where walking is an ordeal.

A magnesium block and striker or a gas lighter is another must for your emergency box. A foil body bag is standard issue for mountain rescue operations and can make a serious contribution to keeping you in good shape until help arrives.

Much of what has been covered here applies only for travellers to the more remote areas, but depending on where you're going, consult your physician for a list of more specific items. A medical kit that can cover almost every eventuality would probably weigh more than your car.

A list of emergency telephone numbers in the area you intend visiting should appear in the front pages of the local telephone directory. When you arrive, jot these down and keep them in your first aid kit in case of emergency.

CHAPTER FIFTEEN

ABLUTIONS AND CAMP ETIQUETTE

ABLUTION BLOCKS

The ablution block is often the central feature of the more established resort. This does not mean that it is right in the middle – it is simply the one place to which everyone goes at some time or other. In the bigger resorts there is usually more than one, and there will be a steady flow of traffic to and from the changing rooms, showers, toilets, laundry and washing-up facilities. You may find queues at crucial times of the day, and although people try to stagger their activities to avoid this, there will be times when you have to come back later. Don't spend more time than you need at these facilities.

The water at most resorts is heated by gas on its way to the tap, as this is the cheapest way of providing an almost endless supply, and gas or electricity is not used up keeping water hot when no one is around. Some resorts do still rely on large-capacity geysers, so get into the habit of using resources sparingly.

Communal cooking or washing-up facilities can become a problem, as they are also very social gathering places. It's easy to get involved in a conversation and not notice that someone else is patiently waiting to wash their dinner plates or clothing. You don't need to stop an interesting conversation, but keep whatever it is you are doing on the move. Remember that others are on holiday too and that their time is as valuable as your own.

Dress discreetly when going between campsite and ablution areas:

a beach gown or wrap-around garment is quite acceptable, but a towel is not! If you seriously offend anyone (and it may be up to them to decide whether or not you have), you may be asked to leave the resort. Without becoming paranoid, try to be sensitive to the general atmosphere.

In the bush, showers are often a bucket or canvas bag up in a tree, and the so-called 'cubicle' is nothing more than an enclosed hessian or reed screen. Do not be alarmed if your feet and head are visible – the fact that your presence is obvious should preserve your dignity.

RIVERSIDE SAFETY

If you are washing in a river, check that it is not home to any of the larger reptiles or mammals. Crocodiles are stealthy predators and can approach to within a metre and still be invisible. Their motionless poses are not a sign of sluggishness, and the slightest contact will see their powerful jaws slamming shut with the speed and ferocity of a steel trap.

Hippos are deceptively comical and are responsible for more deaths than any other animal in Africa. They often crush their victims in their headlong flight to water and safety, but also attack smaller river craft such as dugouts and fibreglass canoes. The large bulls can be extremely aggressive, and their enormous bulk makes them a fearsome adversary. Unless you are heavily armed or have some sure means of escape, avoid confrontation at all costs.

Drinking, or washing clothing in a river is only acceptable if you are using environmentally friendly products. These are readily available and there is no excuse for polluting wild waters with detergents and other contaminants.

For those who don't already know, the bush toilet consists of a toilet roll, a small gardening spade and lots of bush! The use of all three should be quite obvious. Wander as far from the path as you can, and make sure that when you leave, the signs of your passing are as unnoticeable as you can make them.

BUSH ETIQUETTE

Many people go camping to get away from it all, and expect to find the peace and tranquillity they are paying for. If you are visiting a nature or game reserve you can safely assume that everyone who goes there does so to experience the natural environment. You may come across ardent birdwatchers, reptile or plant enthusiasts, amateur astronomers and wannabe entomologists. In-between are people who simply love to wallow in the delightful chaos provided by Our Creator.

In the bush environment, game-viewing is a favourite pastime, so if you see a car full of camera-laden people 'oohing' and 'aahing' over a lion kill, a rare bird or some other once-in-a-lifetime-experience, approach with extreme caution and make every effort not to disturb the proceedings. Someone may have waited years or travelled thousands of kilometres to witness this event, and if you race up noisily in your car you may destroy the moment for everyone, including yourself.

You may well bump into many knowledgeable people at a game park, and by demonstrating a genuine interest you might find out lots of interesting information that does not appear on the brochures: the whereabouts of a particular animal's territory; where a herd was last seen; the best time of day to visit a certain viewpoint. Enthusiasts are always willing to share their knowledge with like-minded people.

MUSIC

At night, the sounds of the bush take on a special significance for many visitors. While music is usually tolerated in small doses, the sound of your favourite rap artist is unlikely to be considered an improvement on five million cicadas, or the mournful sound of a lion roaring in the distance. If you cannot live without music, pack your headphones or play it so that you don't disturb anyone else. Some reserves have banned radios altogether (be sure to check the brochures), and there is no benefit to be had from falling foul of a disturbed naturalist.

Some of the more commercial resorts provide nightly discos, which will be frequented by everyone who likes music and the socialising that goes with it. Christmas and New Year's Eve would not be the same without these events, and if they are well run can be enormous fun for the whole family. Because they happen 'on site', as it were, you do not have to worry about speeding fines or road blocks as you make your way home.

SIMPLE GOOD MANNERS

If you have a caravan or motorhome, make sure the outlet does not funnel your dirty water into your neighbours' site, and don't be shy to point out if theirs does the same to you.

Try not to confront people aggressively, though, as they may be genuinely unaware of what's happening, but there is no sense in suffering in silence when the solution is only syllables away.

If you have children, make sure they know and obey the rules of the resort at all times. Generally speaking, children mix more easily than adults do, and problems tend to be few and far between. Errant behaviour, if and when it occurs, should not be allowed to escalate to the point where it becomes a problem that has to be controlled by others.

Even under perfectly ordinary situations, strangers may feel awkward if they suddenly find a strange child in their midst. If your child goes visiting, check with the hosts that the invitation carries parental consent, and be prepared to reciprocate when you can. Never allow your children to go off with people you have not met or whose activities you disapprove of, and use common sense in allowing juvenile partnerships to form.

Without being deliberately unhelpful, be careful about lending things to others. If you borrow something, be sure to return it as soon as you have finished with it. A helpful neighbour will always appreciate being invited over for coffee and a friendly chat after dinner. When approaching a strange campsite, perhaps to ask for help, make your presence known by a clearly audible greeting, and do not enter their living area unless invited.

Your holidays will be more rewarding – in a surprising number of ways – if you're sensitive to your environment, and your example will help to educate others. Be generous in offering help and gracious in accepting it. Individual contributions may seem insignificant but the collective rewards are immeasurable.

APPENDIX ONE

SHOPS, CLUBS AND MAGAZINES

ACTION AFRICA
Durban (031) 700-4630

**ARMOUR STEEL
(4X4 ACCESSORIES)**
Cape Town (021) 790-1980

**ARMY SURPLUS TENTS
AND EQUIPMENT**
Pretoria (012) 327-1185

**ATLANTA MANUFACTURING
JUMBO JACKS
AND WINCHES**
Pretoria (012) 803-6620/1/2

**BIG COUNTRY
4X4 AND OUTDOOR**
Pretoria (012) 543-1791

**BILSTEIN SHOCK
ABSORBERS**
Johannesburg (011) 493-5730

**B'RAKHAH OFF-ROAD
CAMPERS**
Pretoria (012) 663-4501

**BUSHMAN OFF-ROAD
TRAILERS**
Durban (031) 751-2405

CAMPA TRAILER/CARAVANS
083-440-2211

CAMPERVAN HIRE AND TOURS
Pretoria (012) 981-4666

CAMPING AND OUTDOORS
Durban (031) 579-1950

CARAVAN AND OUTDOOR LIFE
Cape Town (021) 424-1457/8/9

**CONQUEROR SAFARI
TRAILERS**
Free State (051) 9-6533

**CRISTY SPORTS,
TAILOR-MADE TENTS**
Cape Town (021) 712-5020

**CUT SALES OFF-
ROAD TRAILERS**
Gauteng (011) 466-2363

**DESERT WOLF STAINLESS-
STEEL OFF-ROAD TRAILERS**
Pretoria (012) 811-1168

**DIESEL DOG V8 DIESEL
SPECIALIST**
KwaZulu-Natal (0325) 78-5151

ECHO ROOF TOP TENTS
Pretoria (012) 808-2786

EEZI-AWN TENTS
Gauteng (011) 792-1731

**ENGEL AND DESERT COOL
FRIDGES AND FREEZERS**
Gauteng (011) 454-2875

***GETAWAY* MAGAZINE**
Cape Town (021) 530-3100
Gauteng (011) 783-7030

GEYSER 2000
Pretoria (012) 329-1212

**GREENSPORT CAMPING
AND OUTDOOR
South Africa**
Cape Town (021) 52-4458
Namibia
Rundu (067) 25-5669/9
Swakopmund (064) 40-0318
Tsumeb (067) 22-1161
Windhoek (061) 23-4131

HIKER'S PARADISE
Pretoria (012) 365-2053; 663-7647
Durban (031) 701-1654

**THE HOUSE OF HENRY,
CAR SEAT COVERS**
Bloemfontein (051) 4432
Cape Town (021) 424-1412
Durban (031) 332-4628
Port Elizabeth (041) 365-0680
Randburg (011) 886-7601

JURGENS CLUB
Pretoria (012) 421-5107

KARRITE LUGGAGE SYSTEMS
Nationwide 0800-11-35-34

**KENNIS CARAVANS
AND OUTDOOR**
Johannesburg (011) 664-7000

LEATHERMAN KNIVES
Cape Town (021) 975-2700

**THE LEISURE SHOP
Eastern Cape**
East London (0431) 2-3104
Port Elizabeth (041) 51-4355;
   51-5363
Free State
Bethlehem (058) 303-5050
Bloemfontein (051) 430-3831;
   430-3401
Kimberley (053) 861-4865
Welkom (057) 357-3071
Gauteng
Alberton (011) 907-8717
Benoni (011) 973-3747
Boksburg (011) 826-6241
Kempton Park (011) 894-7021;
   974-5595/8

Pretoria (012) 329-2287; 335-2531
Randburg (011) 792-1456
Roodepoort (011) 664-7000
Springs (011) 811-2666
Vereenging (016) 421-1507/9
KwaZulu-Natal
Pietermaritzburg (0331)
 45-5141
Pinetown (031) 72-7291;
 729-326/7/8
Ramsgate (03931/039) 7-9354
Richards Bay (0351) 98-6762
Mpumalanga
Ermelo (017) 9-2502/3
Lydenburg (013) 2371/4
Middelburg (013) 243-5060
Nelspruit (013) 741-1055
Louis Trichardt (015) 638-0402
Witbank (013) 7-5032/3
North-West
Brits (012) 252-5169
Klerksdorp (018) 462-7261
Rustenburg (014) 2-5152
Northern Province
Pietersburg (015) 291-3166
Western Cape
Bellville (021) 993-4841
Goodwood (021) 591-5264
Mossel Bay (0444) 4511
Tygervalley (021) 948-0743
Strand (021) 854-7949

LOFTUS CARAVAN CITY
Johannesburg (011) 792-1456

MAUI SECOND-HAND MOTORHOMES
Gauteng (011) 396-1445

MINUS 40 FRIDGES AND FREEZERS
Pretoria (012) 386-2290

MOSQUITO NETS
Durban (031) 568-1821

MOTORHOME CLUB SA
Cape Town (021) 797-9233;
 988-1123
Durban (031) 764-5438;
 764-5520
Gauteng (012) 462-8407;
 462-8670
Port Elizabeth (041) 586-0632;
 585-2397

NATAL CARAVANS AND MARINE
Durban (031) 72-7291

NATIONAL LUNA LEISURE AND OUTDOOR LIGHTING
Gauteng (011) 452-5438

NATIONAL TENTS AND SAILS
Pretoria (012) 719-9035

NATIONWIDE CRUISER HIRE 4X4
Johannesburg (011) 318-1546

NORTHERN OFF-ROAD EQUIPMENT
Gauteng (011) 791-1611

NYALA TENTS
Gauteng (011) 316-4777

OLD MAN EMU 4X4 SHOCKS AND SUSPENSION
Gauteng (011) 624-3522

OUTDOOR WAREHOUSE
Boksburg (011) 397-3844
Cape Town (021) 948-6221
Durban (031) 263-0851
Randburg (011) 792-8331
Pietersburg (015) 297-7412
Pretoria (012) 661-0505

THE OUTDOORSMAN
Alberton (011) 907-1107
Benoni (011) 422-1610
Durban (031) 25-4454
Pietermaritzburg (0331) 42-8478
Pretoria (012) 328-7167/8
Randburg (011) 787-8316
Vereeniging (016) 422-3582
Witbank (0136) 92-4031

OUT THERE MAGAZINE
Johannesburg (011) 280-5454

OVERLANDER AND BUSHPIG OFF-ROAD TRAILERS
Durban (031) 569-3826

PADDLEYAK SEA KAYAKS
Cape Town (021) 790-5611

PENINSULA CARAVAN CLUB
Cape Town (021) 671-2101

SA CARAVAN ASSOCIATION
Gauteng (011) 823-5917

SA CAMPING CLUB
Cape Town (021) 782-5222
Durban (031) 462-9885
Gauteng (011) 792-1732
Port Elizabeth (041) 73-1833

SAFARI CENTRE 4X4 STORES
Bloemfontein (051) 430-3831
Cape Town (021) 595-3910
Johannesburg (011) 465-3817
Port Elizabeth (041) 374-0800
Pretoria (012) 348-3253

SAFARI GUILD
Benoni (011) 465-4970
Bloemfontein (051) 421-0065
Kempton Park (011) 762-4136
Potchefstroom (0148) 294-6525
Pretoria (012) 76-2388

SKYTOP CANOPIES
Cape Town (021) 551-9050
Johannesburg (011) 609-7890

STORM 4X4 ACCESSORIES
Gauteng (011) 452-6868

TAKLA LOAD LINERS
Gauteng (011) 466-0147

TECHNITOP PRODUCTS, ROOF TOP TENTS, TRAILERS AND STORAGE SYSTEMS
Gauteng (011) 474-2582

**TENTCO TENT MANU-
FACTURERS AND
REPAIRERS**
Boksburg (011) 397-3844

**TJM PRODUCTS
4X4 AND COMMERCIAL
EQUIPMENT**
Vereeniging (016) 362-0431

TRAPEZIUM STABILISERS
Johannesburg (011) 474-4431

**TREKKERS OUTDOOR
RECREATION CLUB**
Cape Town (021) 689-5582

**WAYNE'S 4X4
TECHNOLOGIES
LANDROVER SPECIALISTS**
Pretoria (012) 653-0309

WEBER (BARBEQUES)
Johannesburg (011) 454-2369
Cape Town (021) 982-5107

Telephone numbers correct at time of going to print.

APPENDIX TWO

CARAVAN PARKS

EASTERN CAPE

ADDO ELEPHANT NATIONAL PARK (Addo)	(042) 233-0556
AMATOLA GUEST HOUSE (Hogsback)	(045) 962-1059
ANCHORAGE HOTEL (Umtata)	(047) 534-0061
ANDREW RABIE CARAVAN PARK (Port Elizabeth)	(041) 374-5604
ARENA RIVERSIDE RESORT (East London)	(043) 734-3055
ARENDSNES HOLIDAY RESORT (Cintsa East)	(043) 738-5064
BEACHVIEW HOLIDAY RESORT (Emerald Hill)	(041) 378-1884
BEN MARAIS CARAVAN PARK (Humansdorp)	(042) 295-2429
BEN MCDUI CARAVAN PARK (Barkly East)	(045) 971-0446
BESTERSHOEK CHALETS (Somerset East)	(042) 243-1333
BLANCO GUEST FARM (Tarkastad)	(045) 846-9163
BOESMANSRIVIERMOND PARK (Bushmans River Mouth)	(046) 648-1227
BOSBOKSTRAND RESORT (Tecoma)	(043) 72-4512
CANNON ROCKS RESORT (Cannon Rocks)	(046) 654-0043
CAPE ST FRANCIS RESORT (St Francis Bay)	(042) 298-0054
CEFANI MOUTH RESORT (East London)	(0431) 738-5027
CINTSA EAST RESORT (Cintsa East)	(043) 738-5064
CRADOCK SPA (Cradock)	(048) 881-2709
DE VASSELOT REST CAMP (Tsitsikmamma)	(042) 541-1607
GONUBIE CARAVAN PARK (East London)	(043) 740-4000
GRAHAMSTOWN CARAVAN PARK (Grahamstown)	(0461) 2-9112
HUME PARK RECREATION CLUB (Port Elizabeth)	(041) 55-4013
JOORST CARAVAN PARK (Humewood)	(041) 61-1074
KEI MOUTH CARAVAN PARK (Kei Mouth)	(043) 841-1004
KOLOGHA CARAVAN PARK (Stutterheim)	(0436) 83-2474
LAGOON VALLEY RESORT (East London)	(043) 736-9785
MAITLAND RIVER RESORT (Emerald Hill)	(041) 74-1884
MOLTENO CARAVAN PARK (Molteno)	(04572) 21
MORGAN'S BAY HOTEL (Morgan's Bay)	(043) 841-1062

OCEAN VIEW GUEST FARM (Komga) (043) 831-2140
OCEANVIEW HOLIDAY RESORT (Port Elizabeth) (041) 378-1729
PEARSON PARK RESORT (Colchester) (041) 468-0040
PINE LODGE PORT ELIZABETH (Port Elizabeth) (041) 53-4004
PSA HOLIDAY RESORT (East London) (043) 732-1022
RAINBOW VALLEY RESORT (East London) (043) 748-4519
RIVERSIDE CARAVAN PARK (Port Alfred) (046) 624-2230
ROEBERT'S HOLIDAY RESORT (East London) (043) 736-7035
SEA ACRES HOLIDAY RESORT (Humewood) (041) 583-3095
STORMS RIVER MOUTH CAMP (Stormsrivier) (042) 541-1607
TSITSIKAMMA NATIONAL PARK (Stormsriver) (042) 541-1607
VAN STADENS RIVER MOUTH (Van Stadens River) (041) 776-1059
WILLOWS CARAVAN PARK (Port Alfred) (046) 624-5201
WILLOWS HOLIDAY RESORT (Humewood) (041) 366-1717
WOODY CAPE RESORT (Alexandria) (046) 654-0219
YELLOW SANDS CARAVAN PARK (East London) (043) 734-3043

FREE STATE

ARIZONA GAME LODGE (Senekal) (058) 481-2547
AVENTURA ALDAM (Ventersburg) (057) 652-2200
AVENTURA MASELSPOORT (Bloemfontein) (051) 441-7848
AVENTURA MIDWATERS (Gariep Dam) (051) 754-0045
BETHULIE DAM RESORT (Bethulie) (051762) 2
BIETJIEWATER RESORT (Reitz) (058) 863-3028
DAGBREEK RESORT (Bloemfontein) (051) 33-2490
EEUFEES CARAVAN PARK (Zastron) (051) 673-1397
ERFENIS DAM NATURE RESERVE (Theunissen) (05772) 4211
HARRISMITH CARAVAN PARK (Harrismith) (058) 622-3525
KLEIN PARADYS RESORT (Parys) (056) 818-1214
KROONPARK HOLIDAY RESORT (Kroonstad) (0562) 3-1942
LELIEHOEK RESORT (Ladybrand) (05191) 4-0260
LOCH ATHLONE RESORT (Bethlehem) (058) 303-4981
MATWABENG CARAVAN PARK (Senekal) (05848) 2142
MEIRINGSKLOOF PARK (Fouriesburg) (058) 223-0067
MIMOSA CARAVAN PARK (Odendaalsrus) (057) 354-1222
MOUNT EVEREST GAME RESERVE (Harrismith) (058) 622-3433
PHILIP SANDERS RESORT (Bloemfontein) (051) 441-7611
PRESIDENT BRAND PARK (Harrismith) (058) 622-3525

CARAVAN PARKS

RIVERVIEW COUNTRY INN (Swinburne) (058) 671-1033
RUSTFONTEIN DAM RESORT (Bloemspruit) (051) 526-2970
SENEKAL CARAVAN PARK (Senekal) (05848) 2142
SMILIN' THRU RESORT (Parys) (056) 816-2200
STERKFONTEIN DAM RESERVE (Harrismith) (058) 622-3520
THOM PARK CARAVAN PARK (Ficksburg) (051) 933-2122
TIKWE LODGE (Virginia) (057) 212-3306
TOM'S PLACE (near Bloemfontein) (05215) 680
TUSSEN DIE RIVIERE NATURE RESERVE
  (Bethulie) (051) 763-1114
UNIEFEESDAM CARAVAN PARK (Heilbron) (05889) 2-2014
VREDE MARINA (Vrede) (01334) 3-2080
WATERPARK CARAVAN PARK (Frankfort) (0588) 31-0519
WINBURG CARAVAN PARK (Winburg) (05242) 3

GAUTENG
AVENTURA KAREEKLOOF (Meyerton) (016) 365-5334
AVENTURA ROODEPLAATDAM (Lynn East) (012) 808-5078
BENTLEY'S COUNTRY LODGE (Pretoria North) (012) 542-1751
DOORNKLOOF CARAVAN PARK (Irene) (012) 667-1176
EMFULENI CARAVAN PARK (Vanderbijlpark) (016) 932-3683
FISHERMAN'S FRIEND RESORT (Lynn East) (012) 808-0349
FORTUNA RESORT (Balfour) (017) 773-1489
FOUNTAINS VALLEY (Pretoria) (012) 44-7131
JIM FOUCHÉ HOLIDAY RESORT (Vaal Dam) (016) 351-1719
KARAPARK (Edenvale) (011) 453-0301
KIEWIET CARAVAN PARK (Onderstepoort) (012) 561-1475
KOPPISOL CLUB RESORT (De Deur) (016) 556-1112
LOVERS' ROCK (Magaliesburg) (014) 577-1327
MAR-LEO CARAVAN PARK (Lynn East) (012) 808-0236
MURRAY PARK (Springs) (011) 816-1104
NGONYAMA LION LODGE (Krugersdorp) (011) 953-1511
NKWE CARAVAN PARK (Lynwood Ridge) (012) 811-0095
OMARAMBA HOLIDAY RESORT (near Pretoria) (014) 572-3004
POLKADRAAI CARAVAN PARK
  (Voortrekkerhoogte) (012) 666-8710
RIEBEECK LAKE CARAVAN PARK (Randfontein) (011) 411-0184
ZEMVELO GAME PARK (Bronkhorstspruit) (013) 932-2211

KWAZULU-NATAL

ALBERT FALLS RESERVE (Cramond)	(033) 569-1202
AMCOR CARAVAN PARK (Newcastle)	(03431) 8-1273
BALELE RECREATION RESORT (Utrecht)	(03433) 3041
BENDIGO CARAVAN PARK (Anerley)	(039) 681-3451
BERGVILLE CARAVAN PARK (Drakensberg)	(036) 448-1273
CAPE VIDAL (St Lucia Estuary)	(035) 590-1404
CARAVAN COVE (Park Rynie)	(039) 976-1215
CASA BENRI CARAVAN PARK (Mtunzini)	(0353) 40-1997
CASTAWAYS HOLIDAY RESORT (Munster)	(03930) 9-2574
CHARLES HOFFE CARAVAN PARK (Scottburgh)	(039) 976-0651
COBHAM (Drakensberg)	(033) 702-0831
DE WET CARAVAN PARK (Margate)	(039) 312-1022
DOLPHIN HOLIDAY RESORT (Ballito)	(0322) 6-2187
DRAGON PEAKS RESORT (Drakensberg)	(036) 468-1031
DRAKENSVILLE RESORT (Drakensberg)	(036) 438-6287
DUNDEE CARAVAN PARK (Dundee)	(0341) 8-2486
EAGLE'S NEST CARAVAN PARK (Howick)	(0332) 30-2797
ESTCOURT CARAVAN PARK (Estcourt)	(0363) 2-3000
FALSE BAY PARK (Hluhluwe village)	(035) 562-0425
FANIE'S ISLAND (Mtubatuba)	(035) 550-1631
HAPPY DAYS CHALETS (Hibberdene)	(039) 699-2310
HAPPY WANDERERS HOLIDAY RESORT (Kelso)	(039) 975-1104
HARBOUR LIGHTS RESORT (Empangeni)	(0351) 96-6239
HAZELMERE NATURE RESORT (Umdloti)	(0322) 33-2315
HIBBERDENE CARAVAN PARK (Hibberdene)	(039699) 2308
HIDEAWAY CARAVAN PARK (Umzumbe)	(039) 684-6283
HIGHMOOR NATURE RESERVE (Drakensberg)	(033) 263-7240
HILLSIDE CAMP (Drakensberg)	(0363) 33-6255
HIMEVILLE NATURE RESERVE (Drakensberg)	(033) 702-1036
HLALANATHI RESORT (Drakensberg)	(036) 438-6308
IILANGA HOLIDAY RESORT (Anerley)	(0391) 8-3280
ILLOVO BEACH HOLIDAY PARK (Illovo Beach)	(031) 916-3472
INJASUTI CAMP (Drakensberg)	(036) 488-1050
JACARANDA LODGE (Louwsberg)	(0388) 7-5200
KARRIDENE PROTEA HOTEL (Illovo)	(031) 916-7228
KELSO VALLEY CARAVAN PARK (Pennington)	(039) 975-1805
KELVIN GROVE FARM (Drakensberg)	(036) 488-1652

CARAVAN PARKS

KINGFISHER CARAVAN PARK (Shelly Beach)	(039) 315-0272
KLIPFONTEIN DAM CARAVAN PARK (Vryheid)	(0381) 81-2133
KOKSTAD CARAVAN PARK (Kokstad)	(037) 727-2141
LA MOUETTE CARAVAN PARK (Stanger)	(0324) 2-2547
LAKE MERTHLEY CARAVAN PARK (Greytown)	(0334) 3-1171
LEISURE VIEW CARAVAN PARK (Port Edward)	(03930) 9-2367
MAC NICOLS BAZLEY RESORT (Scottburgh)	(039) 977-8863
MAC NICOLS PENNINGTON (Pennington)	(039) 975-1107
MAHAI CAMP (Drakensberg)	(036) 438-6303
MAPELANE NATURE RESERVE (St Lucia)	(035) 590-1407
MARGATE CARAVAN PARK (Margate)	(039) 312-0852
MARLON HOLIDAY RESORT (Anerley)	(039) 681-3596
MIDMAR NATURE RESERVE (Howick)	(0332) 30-2067
MITTENWALD CARAVAN PARK (Munster)	(039) 319-1180
MONK'S COWL CARAVAN PARK (Drakensberg)	(036) 468-1103
MONZI CARAVAN PARK (Mtubatuba)	(035) 550-1601
MOUNTAIN SPLENDOUR (Drakensberg)	(036) 468-1172
MSUNDUZI CARAVAN PARK (Oribi)	(0331) 6-5342
MTWALUME CARAVAN PARK (Mtwalume)	(039) 972-1719
OASIS CARAVAN PARK (Uvongo)	(039) 315-0778
OCEAN CALL CARAVAN PARK (Winkelspruit)	(031) 916-2644
OLD PONT HOLIDAY RESORT (Port Edward)	(039) 313-2211
OOTEEKALIA RESORT (Southbroom)	(03931) 6080
PARADISE HOLIDAY RESORT (Southbroom)	(039) 313-0655
PAULPIETERSBURG CARAVAN PARK (Paulpietersburg)	(038) 995-1650
PEATTIES' LAKESIDE RESORT (near Pietermaritzburg)	(033) 569-0536
PHAMBUKA (Kosi Bay estuary)	(035) 591-0052
PONGOLA CARAVAN PARK (Pongola)	(03441) 3-1789
PORT O' CALL CARAVAN PARK (Margate)	(039) 313-0511
PRAIRIE PARK RESORT (Anerley)	(039) 681-2013
PUMLANI CARAVAN & CAMPING PARK (Margate)	(039) 312-0482
RIVERBANK CARAVAN PARK (Mooi River)	(0333) 3-2144
ROCKY BAY CARAVAN PARK (Park Rynie)	(039) 972-0546
RUGGED GLEN (Drakensberg)	(036) 438-6303
RYNIE HILL PARK (Park Rynie)	(039) 978-3243
SALT ROCK HOTEL (Salt Rock)	(0322) 525-5025
SCOTTBURGH CARAVAN PARK (Scottburgh)	(039) 976-0291
SILVERSTREAMS CARAVAN PARK (Drakensberg)	(033) 701-1249

SODWANA BAY NATIONAL PARK (Sodwana Bay) (035) 571-0051
SPIOENKOP NATURE RESERVE (Drakensberg) (036) 488-1578
SUGARLOAF CARAVAN PARK (St Lucia) (035) 590-1340
TUGELA MOUTH CARAVAN PARK (Mandeni) (032) 458-4170
TUZIGAZI CARAVAN PARK (Richards Bay) (0351) 3-1971
UMDONI CARAVAN RESORT (Pennington) (039) 975-1261
UMLALAZI NATURE RESERVE (Mtunzini) (0353) 40-1836
UMTENTWENI CARAVAN PARK (Sea Park) (039) 695-0531
VILLA SPA RESORT (Illovo Beach) (031) 916-4939
VRYHEID CARAVAN PARK (Vryheid) (0381) 81-2133
WAGENDRIFT NATURE RESERVE (Estcourt) (036) 352-5520
WEENEN NATURE RESERVE (Weenen) (0363) 4-1809
WHITE MOUNTAIN LODGE (Estcourt) (036) 353-3437
WINKELSPRUIT CARAVAN PARK (Winkelspruit) (031) 916-1720
XAXAZA CARAVAN PARK (Mtunzini) (0353) 40-1843
ZINKWAZI HOLIDAY RESORT (Stanger) (032) 485-3344

MPUMALANGA
AVENTURA ECO BLYDEPOORT (Ohrigstad) (013) 769-8005
AVENTURA ECO LOSKOPDAM (Middelburg) (013) 262-3064
AVENTURA SPA BADPLAAS (Badplaas) (017) 844-1020
BARBERTON CARAVAN PARK (Barberton) (013) 712-3323
BELFAST DAM RESORT (Belfast) (01325) 3-1121
BERG-EN-DAL CAMP (Kruger National Park) (013) 735-6106
COME TOGETHER GUEST FARM (Schagen) (013) 733-3052
DIMALACHITE HOLIDAY RESORT (Witbank) (056) 818-1860
ELANDSKRANS RESORT (Waterval Boven) (013) 257-0175
GRASKOP HOLIDAY RESORT (Graskop) (013) 767-1126
GROBLERSDAL CARAVAN PARK (Groblersdal) (013) 262-3056
IN DA BUNDU (Belfast) (013) 253-0928
JOCK OF THE BUSHVELD (Kruger National Park) (013) 764-2178
KUDU LODGE (Nelspruit) (013) 726-0080
LEISURE TIME CARAVAN PARK (Standerton) (017) 712-2256
LOWER SABIE CAMP (Kruger National Park) (013) 735-6056
MALELANE CAMP (Kruger National Park) (013) 735-6152
MARULANI KLOOF LODGE (Middelburg) (013) 262-4016
MERRY PEBBLES (Sabie) (013) 764-2266
MOOLMAN HOTEL (Moolman) (017) 821-0731

MOUNTAIN TROUT PARK (Carolina) (017) 843-2088
NUMBI HOTEL (Hazyview) (013) 737-7301
PANORAMA REST CAMP (Graskop) (013) 767-1091
PHELWANA GAME LODGE (Kiepersol) (015) 793-2475
PIET RETIEF CARAVAN PARK (Piet Retief) (01782) 2211
PILGRIM'S REST PARK (Pilgrim's Rest) (013) 768-1367
POLKA DOT CARAVAN PARK (Nelspruit) (013) 755-6173
PRETORIUSKOP CAMP (Kruger National Park) (013) 735-5128
SAFUBI RIVER LODGE & PARK (Nelspruit) (013) 741-3253
SIESTA HOLIDAY RESORT (Lydenburg) (013) 235-2886
SKUKUZA CAMP (Kruger National Park) (013) 735-5611
WITBANK RECREATION RESORT (Witbank) (0135) 7-0151

NORTH-WEST

ABJATERSKOP HOTEL (Zeerust) (018) 642-2008
AMERSFOORT CARAVAN PARK (Amersfoort) (017) 753-1006
AMIGO'S CARAVAN PARK (Ventersdorp) (018) 264-2433
ANANDA COUNTRY LODGE (Rustenburg) (014) 597-1966
ATKV BUFFELSPOORT RESORT (Marikana) (014) 572-3214
AVENTURA VAAL SPA (Christiana) (053) 441-2244
BARBERSPAN HOTEL & RESORT (Delareyville) (053) 948-1930
BERGHEIM HOLIDAY RESORT (Kroondal) (014) 537-2363
BOEREPLAAS HOLIDAY RESORT (Vryburg) (05391) 7-1248
CHATEAU RONDEAU RESORT (Brits) (012) 253-0394
HARTBEESHOEK NATURE RESERVE (Brits) (012) 251-1807
HENNOPS PRIDE RESORT (Erasmia) (012) 659-0043
KLEIN MARICO POORT (Zeerust) (018) 646-0141
KLERKSDORP DAM RESORT (Klerksdorp) (018) 462-7210
KLOOF HOLIDAY RESORT (Rustenburg) (014) 594-1037
KOKORIBA GAME RESERVE (Brits) (012) 277-1940
LAKE RECREATION RESORT (Noordbrug) (018) 299-5470
MANYANE CARAVAN PARK (Rustenburg) (014) 555-6135
OBERON PLEASURE RESORT (Hartbeespoort) (01205) 5-1353
ORKNEY VAAL RESORT (Klerksdorp) (018) 473-3228
SWARTFONTEIN RESORT (Vryburg) (053) 91-4825
WATERPARADISE CARAVAN PARK (Klerksdorp) (018) 464-2917
WAWIELPARK HOLIDAY RESORT (Stilfontein) (018) 441-1093

NORTHERN CAPE

ALEXKOR/BRANDKAROS (Alexander Bay)	(0256) 831-1856
AUGRABIES FALLS PARK (Augrabies)	(054) 451-0050
BARKLY WEST RESORT (Barkly West)	(053) 531-0671
CALVINIA CARAVAN PARK (Calvinia)	(0273) 41-1011
DIE BOS VAKANSIEOORD (Prieska)	(0594) 6-1059
DIE EILAND HOLIDAY RESORT (Upington)	(054) 334-0286
GARIES CARAVAN PARK (Garies)	(027) 65-2101
GRIEKWASTAD CARAVAN PARK (Griekwastad)	(05962) 19
HARTSWATER CARAVAN PARK (Hartswater)	(053) 474-0143
JWH DU PLESSIS PARK (Port Nolloth)	(0255) 8706
KALAHARI GEMSBOK NATIONAL PARK (near Upington)	(054) 561-0021
KAMBRO ACCOMMODATION (Britstown)	(083) 305-6668
KAMIESKROON HOTEL (Kamieskroon)	(027) 672-1614
KANONEILAND RESORT (Kanoneiland)	(054) 491-1223
KEIMOES CARAVAN PARK (Keimoes)	(054) 461-1016
KHEI APPEL RESORT (Kathu)	(05376) 3-2261
KIMBERLEY PLEASURE RESORT (Barkly West)	(053) 531-0626
KOKERBOOM MOTEL (Springbok)	(0251) 2-2685
KURUMAN CARAVAN PARK (Kuruman)	(053) 712-1479
OASIS CARAVAN PARK (De Aar)	(053) 631-0927 (ext) 253
OPEN MINE CARAVAN PARK (Kimberley)	(0531) 80-6911
PRIESKA CARAVAN PARK (Prieska)	(0594) 6-1002
RUS 'N BIETJIE (Pofadder)	(02532) 36
SPRINGBOK CARAVAN PARK (Springbok)	(0251) 8-1584
VAN DER MERWE CARAVAN PARK (De Aar)	(053) 631-9271
VAN ZYLSVLEI CARAVAN PARK (Colesberg)	(051) 753-0589
VANDERKLOOF RESORT (Vanderkloof)	(053) 664-0198
VICTORIA WEST CARAVAN PARK (Victoria West)	(053) 621-0413
VOORTREKKER CARAVAN PARK (Canarvon)	(053) 382-3012

NORTHERN PROVINCE

AVENTURA ECO EILAND (Letsitele)	(015) 386-8667
AVENTURA ECO SWADINI (Hoedspruit)	(015) 795-5141
AVENTURA ECO TSHIPISE (Tshipise)	(015539) 624
AVENTURA SPA WARMBATHS (Warmbaths)	(014) 736-2200
BALULE CAMP (Kruger National Park)	(013) 735-6606
BAOBAB CARAVAN PARK (Messina)	(015) 534-3504

CARAVAN PARKS

BEN ALBERTS NATURE RESERVE (Thabazimbi)	(014) 777-1670
BEN LAVIN NATURE RESERVE (Louis Trichardt)	(015) 516-4534
BOTHANIA HILLS (Naboomspruit)	(014) 743-1640
BUKANE GAME FARM (Nylstroom)	(014) 717-1053
DIE OOG HOT SPRING RESORT (Naboomspruit)	(014) 743-0267
DUIWELSKLOOF RESORT (Tzaneen)	(015) 309-9651
EUROSUN CARAVAN PARK (Nylstroom)	(014) 717-1328
FAIRVIEW COUNTRY LODGE (Tzaneen)	(015) 307-2679
GROOTKLIP CARAVAN PARK (Louis Trichardt)	(015) 516-4886
HIPPO POOLS RESORT (Hoedspruit)	(015) 793-2088
HONEYGUIDE TENTED SAFARI CAMP (Manyeleti Reserve)	(011) 483-2734
LANTANA LODGE (Phalaborwa)	(0157) 81-5191
LETABA CAMP (Kruger National Park)	(013) 735-6636
LINGA LONGA HOLIDAY FARM (Warmbaths)	(014) 736-4300
LOUIS TRICHARDT CARAVAN PARK (Louis Trichardt)	(015) 516-0212
MABALINGWE NATURE RESERVE (Warmbaths)	(0147) 36-2334
MANOUTSA PARK RESORT (Hoedspruit)	(015) 795-5125
MOPANI CAMP (Kruger National Park)	(013) 735-6536
MORETELE CAMP (Thabazimbi)	(011) 465-5423
PITJANE CAMP (Thabazimbi)	(011) 465-5423
PUNDA MARIA CAMP (Kruger National Park)	(013) 735-6873
RHEMARDO HOLIDAY RESORT (Naboomspruit)	(014) 743-0612
RONWIL HOLIDAY FLATS (Warmbaths)	(014) 736-2350
SATARA REST CAMP (Kruger National Park)	(013) 735-6306
SHINGWEDZI CAMP (Kruger National Park)	(013) 735-6806
STIL 'N RUSTIG (Naboomspruit)	(014) 743-2337
STOKKIESDRAAI RESORT (Nylstroom)	(014) 717-4005
TAMBOTI CAMP (Kruger National Park)	(013) 735-6355
TIBANI LODGE (Potgietersrus)	(015) 491-5609
TREKKERSRUS (Phalaborwa)	(015) 781-5429
UNION PARK CARAVAN PARK (Pietersburg)	(0152) 295-2011
WATERBERG NATUURPRAAL (Vaalwater)	(012) 253-0436
WEESGERUS HOLIDAY RESORT (Nylstroom)	(014) 715-2037

WESTERN CAPE

ALGERIA CAMPING SITE (Cedarberg)	(027) 482-2812
ALLANDALE COTTAGES (Tokai)	(021) 75-3320
ARCH ROCK CARAVAN PARK (Plettenberg Bay)	(04457) 9409

ATKV GOUDINI SPA (Rawsonville) (023) 349-3013
ATKV HARTENBOS RESORT (Hartenbos) (0444) 95-0110
AVENTURA ECO PLETTENBERG (Plettenberg Bay) (04457) 9309
BEAUFORT WEST CARAVAN PARK (Beaufort West) (0201) 2800
BERG RIVER RESORT (Suider-Paarl) (021) 863-1650
BONTEBOK NATIONAL PARK (Swellendam) (028) 514-2735
BRIGADOON CARAVAN PARK (George) (044) 889-0034
BUFFELS BAY CARAVAN PARK (Knysna) (0443) 83-0045
BUFFELSJACHTSBAAI CARAVAN PARK (Bredasdorp) (02848) 2-1852
BUFFELSKOP CARAVAN PARK (Knysna) (044) 383-0045
BULSHOEKDAM RESORT (Clanwilliam) (027) 482-2635
CALITZDORP SPA (Oudtshoorn) (044) 213-3371
CANGO MOUNTAIN RESORT (Oudtshoorn) (044) 272-4506
CEDARBERG RESORT (Cedarberg) (027) 482-2825
CEDARBERG TOURIST PARK (Cedarberg) (027) 482-2807
CHAPMAN'S PEAK PARK (Noordhoek) (021) 789-1225
CITRUSDAL CARAVAN PARK (Citrusdal) (022) 921-3145
CLANWILLIAM DAM RESORT (Clanwilliam) (027) 482-2133
DE BAKKE/SANTOS RESORT (Mossel Bay) (0444) 91-2915
DE DAM HOLIDAY RESORT (Bredasdorp) (02848) 2-1710
DE HOEK MOUNTAIN RESORT (Oudtshoorn) (044) 272-8241
DENNEHOF RESORT (Villiersdorp) (028) 840-2091
DUNE PARK RESORT (Plettenberg Bay) (044) 535-9606
DWARSKERSBOS RESORT (Velddrif) (02288) 4-0110
ELANDS BAY CARAVAN PARK (Piketberg) (0265) 745
ELLENSRUST CARAVAN PARK (Still Bay) (02934) 4-1034
FISH HOEK CARAVAN PARK (Fish Hoek) (021) 782-5503
GANSBAAI CARAVAN PARK (Gansbaai) (028) 384-0111
GEORGE TOURIST RESORT (George) (044) 874-5205
GIFBERG CARAVAN PARK (Vanrhynsdorp) (02727) 9-1287
GLENTANA CARAVAN PARK (George) (044) 879-1536
HARDEKRAALTJIE CARAVAN PARK (Bellville) 021) 948-7225
HENDON PARK RESORT (Gordon's Bay) (021) 856-1324
IMHOFF CARAVAN PARK (Kommetjie) (021) 783-1634
ISLAND LAKE RESORT (Wilderness) (044) 877-1194
KAROO NATIONAL PARK (Beaufort West) (0201) 5-2828
KEURBOOMS LAGOON (Plettenberg Bay) (044) 533-2567
KLEINMOND CARAVAN PARK (Kleinmond) (028) 271-4010

CARAVAN PARKS

KLEINPLAAS RESORT (Oudtshoorn)	(044) 272-5811
KLIPRIVER PARK RESORT (Tulbagh)	(0236) 30-0506
L'AGULHAS CARAVAN PARK (L'Agulhas)	(02846) 5-6015
LAKE BRENTON RESORT (Knynsa)	(0445) 81-0060
LAKE PLEASANT RESORT (Sedgefield)	(044) 343-1985
LANDFALL HOLIDAY RESORT (Sedgefield)	(044) 343-1840
LOOTS CARAVAN PARK (Touws River)	(023) 358-1049
MALMESBURY CARAVAN PARK (Malmesbury)	(0224) 2-3266
MILLER'S POINT RESORT (Simon's Town)	(021) 786-1142
MONK'S CARAVAN PARK (Knysna)	(044) 382-2609
MOORREESBURG CARAVAN PARK (Moorreesburg)	(0264) 3-2246
MOUNTAIN BREEZE (Stellenbosch)	(021) 880-0200
MOUNTAIN SPRING FARM (Albertinia)	(028) 735-2201
NA SMIT TOURIST RESORT (Oudtshoorn)	(044) 272-4152
NEKKIES HOLIDAY RESORT (Worcester)	(023) 343-2909
NUWEPARK (Langebaan)	(022) 772-2442
OATLANDS HOLIDAY VILLAGE (Simon's Town)	(021) 786-1410
ONRUS RIVER RESORT (Onrus River)	(0283) 6-1210
OU SKIP CARAVAN PARK (Melkbosstrand)	(021) 553-2058
OUTENIQUA CARAVAN PARK (Little Brak River)	(044) 696-6089
PALMIET CARAVAN PARK (Kleinmond)	(028) 271-4010
PEARLY BEACH RESORT (Gansbaai)	(02834) 9613
PELICAN HOLIDAY FLATS (Velddrif)	(02288) 3-0383
PINE CREEK CARAVAN PARK (Great Brak River)	(0446) 20-2434
PINE FOREST RESORT (Ceres)	(023) 316-1882
PW KOORTS CARAVAN PARK (Piketberg)	(0261) 3-1126
RIVERSIDE FARM RESORT (Still Bay)	(02934) 4-1608
RIVERSIDE HOLIDAY RESORT (Klein Brak River)	(044) 696-6061
ROBBERG CARAVAN PARK (Plettenberg Bay)	(04457) 3-2571
SAAR GARISCH CARAVAN PARK (Ladismith)	(028) 551-1000
SALDANHA HOLIDAY RESORT (Saldanha Bay)	(022) 701-7000
SALMONSDAM NATURE RESERVE (Hermanus)	(0283) 77-0062
SAN MARINO CARAVAN PARK (Plettenberg Bay)	(04457) 9700
SANDDRIF HOLIDAY RESORT (Clanwilliam)	(027) 482-2825
SEA GLIMPSE HOLIDAY RESORT (George)	(044) 871-1583
STEENBERGS COVE HOTEL (St Helena Bay)	(022) 736-1164
STRANDFONTEIN PARK (Doring Bay)	(02723) 5-1169
STRUISBAAI CARAVAN PARK (Struisbaai)	(02846) 5-6538

STYWELYNE CARAVAN PARK (Velddrif)   (02288) 3-0408
TABAKBAAI HOLIDAY RESORT (Vredenburg)   (022) 714-2248
TAKKIESKLOOF TOURIST CAMP (Riverdale)   (02933) 3-2420
THE BATHS (Citrusdal)   (022) 921-3609
UILENKRAALSMOND PARK (Gansbaai)   (02834) 8-0200
VANRHYNSDORP CARAVAN PARK (Vanrhynsdorp)   (02727) 9-1287
VOORTREKKER PARK (Strand)   (021) 850-4169
WAENHUISKRANS PARK (Arniston)   (02847) 5-9620
WELLINGTON CARAVAN PARK (Wellington)   (021) 873-2603
WILDERNESS NATIONAL PARK (Wilderness)   (044) 877-1197
WOODBOURNE HOLIDAY RESORT (Knysna)   (044) 384-0316
YZERFONTEIN CARAVAN PARK (Yzerfontein)   (02245) 211
ZANDVLEI CARAVAN PARK (Muizenberg)   (021) 788-7881
ZONNEKUS HOLIDAY RESORT (Milnerton)   (021) 972-1833

Telephone numbers correct at time of going to print.

INDEX

Ablution blocks 10, 122–3
air conditioning 22, 45
air mattresses 92
alcohol stoves 70
army tents 27–28
awnings 46

Backpacks 100–101
batteries 59
bicycles 58
bites 118–9
bottle-opener 81
braai units 106–7
brake fluid 60
braking 53
bungalows 11
bush camps 12–3

Camper units 55–6
camper 'vans' 56
camping 23
camping clubs 126–9
candles 61–2
caravan parks 13
    Eastern Cape 131–2
    Free State 132–3
    Gauteng 133
    KwaZulu-Natal 134–6

Mpumalanga 136–7
Northern Cape 138
Northern Province 138–9
North-West 137
Western Cape 139–42
caravans 36–54
colour 40
four-berth 38–9
kitchen area 42–3
power source 41–2
second-hand 40–1
setting-up 37
sleeping in 44
storage space 39–40
tents 45–7
two-berth 37–8
windows 40–1
Caravette II 38
car-top tents 28
chairs 74–5, 105–6
chalets 11
charcoal 90
children's tents 24
clothing 95–98
Coleman pressure lamp 63
cooker tops 67
cooking facilities 10

cooking grids 81–3
cooler boxes 72, 108
cottage tents 24
crockery 85–6
cross-winds 48

Diesel engines 55
dome tents 25–6

Egg-lifter 81
electricity 64

Fire 87–91
    extinguishers 41–2
firearms 15
first-aid kit 119–20
fly sheets 26
foam mats 93
food items 101–2
footwear 96–7
frame tents 26–7, 28
freezers 71–2
fridges 71–72
    portable 71, 108
fuel, storage of 103

Galley 42–3
gas 67, 68
    bottles 48
    lamps 64, 65

stoves, fixed 66, 68
stoves, portable 67
gear ratios 50
geysers 45
ground sheets 47
guy ropes 27

Hammocks 93
hats 95–6
hobs 43
holiday, budgeting 9
holiday planning 8–16
hurricane lamps 62

Jackets 96
jockey wheel 31

Knives 77–8, 80, 81

Light sticks 65
lighting 61–5
lilos 92
long-distance travel 17
Low Pressure Gas (LPG) 63, 66
luggage racks, trailer 36, 34

Malaria 118
mantles, gas lamps 64

143

maps 22
melamine 76
microwaves 42
mosquito netting 41, 47
motorbikes 58
motorhome club 128
motorhomes 55–60
mountain camps
    12–13
mudguards, trailer 34

National parks 12 *see*
    also regional entries
    under caravan parks
no-pressure stoves
    69–71
nose cones 31

Outdoor cooking
    81–91
outdoor kitchen
    66–91
overtaking 53–4

Paper plates 75–6
paraffin 62
    stoves 69–70
photography 20–21
plants, poisonous 119
pop-tops 44, 56
potjies 83–5
power steering 57
pressure lamps 62–3
pressure stoves 67–9
Primus stoves 69
privacy 11
    caravans 44
punctures 33

Red tide 119–20
refrigerators 43
resorts 10–11, 16
    booking 13–14
Richtersveld National
    Park 13

Safari guild 129
safari trailer 34
safety 61, 89, 111,
    112, 121
salad spoons 81
shade 45
shellfish 119
shock absorbers 49
shops, camping equip-
    ment 126–30
skottel 67, 85
sleeping 92–4
sleeping bags 93–4
snack makers 84
snakes 116–7
spares 16, 64
spirit jelly 71
Sprite 38
stabiliser bars 49
stainless steel 86
    plates 76
stings 118–9
storage space 39–40,
    99–103
stoves 66–71
    solid-fuel 71
stretchers 93
sun screens 21
sun umbrellas 104–5
sunscreen 114
survival 116–121

suspension 49–50
    trailer 33
swivel chair 57

Tables 73–4, 105–106
tableware 75–77
tailgates, trailer 35
tents 23–9
    pegs 28–9
    pitching 27
    plastic skirts 46–7
    repair kit 29
    storage of 29
tips
    braking 53
    caravan checklist 46
    caravan packing 48
    caravan second-
        hand 36
    cooking 68
    cooking grids 82–3
    fire making 87–91
    freezers 72
    gas lamps 63–4
    gas leaks 68
    maximum torque 51
    motorhome care
        59–60
    overtaking 53–4
    packing 99–100, 109
    photography 20–1
    reversing 32–3
    safety 61, 89, 111,
        112, 121
    salt storage 77
    tent buying 29
    tent storage 29
    towing 48–54

trailer steering 32–3
vehicle batteries
    59–60
weight 109
torches 64–5
torque 51
trailers 30–5
travelling 17–22
    with children 19–22,
        110–115
    distances 14
    road view 48–9
    sleeping 22
    staying awake 18
trunks, metal 101
tyres 59

UV-protection 97–8

Vehicle
    mirrors 49
    refuelling 9
    servicing 14
    speed 50–3
    ventilation 45

Washing machines 107
washing-up facilities 10
water 102–3
    in caravans 44–5
wheels, trailer 33
wilderness camps
    12–13
wind 52
windbreaks 87, 105
wood 87–90

Zip locks, tents 29